Wish
for the
World

A Daily Meditation for Personal & Planetary Peace

KEREN CLARK POSEY
with
ETHAN & DYSON POSEY

Blue Dolphin Publishing

Published by Blue Dolphin Publishing, Inc.
P.O. Box 8, Nevada City, CA 95959
Orders: 1-800-643-0765
Web: www.bluedolphinpublishing.com

ISBN: 1-57733-132-X

Library of Congress Cataloging-in-Publication Data

Posey, Keren Clark, 1959-
  Wish for the world : a daily meditation for personal & plantetary
peace / Keren Clark Posey with Ethan & Dyson Posey.
      p. cm.
  Includes bibliographical references.
  ISBN 1-57733-132-X (pbk. : alk. paper)
  1. Peace—religious aspects. 2. Prayers for peace. 3. Peace—Meditations. 4. Prayers. 5. Wishes. I. Posey, Ethan, 1992- II. Posey, Dyson,
1992- III. Title.

  BL65.P4P67 2005
  204'.32—dc22

                                                    2004021617

A portion of the profits from the sale of this book will be donated to charity.
wishfortheworld.com

Back cover photo: Sadie K. Posey
Cover and text illustrations: Bret Blevins / optimisticstudios.com

Printed in the United States of America

10   9   8   7   6   5   4   3   2   1

In memory of my parents
Helen "Zipper" Hardin Clark and Donald Wrigley Clark,
who always believed in my ability
to make my dreams and wishes come true.

Introduction

I have always taken solace in the spiritual, questing to find a spiritual practice that suited me. My family was Protestant. I was confirmed in the neighborhood Congregationalist church and, as a teenager, was involved in the youth group. I retain a deep sense of comfort from that church and from what I learned there. However, in studying other religions, particularly Tibetan Buddhism and several types of Shamanism, I have found great teachings and practices that succor me as well.

Since the birth of my twin sons in 1992 and the subsequent arrival of their sister in 1997, I have wondered how best to teach my children about religions and spirituality. Ethan, Dyson and Sadie attend a grammar school with a Waldorf philosophy. While not being "religious," Waldorf education emphasizes the natural-ness of children and the cycles of the seasons and celebrates both with lovely ceremonies. Between the ages of three and five, the boys attended a Christian preschool. At home, we have discus-sions about the Buddha, Jesus and other great spiritual teachers.

Their father and I share with our children our thoughts about concepts such as personal integrity, compassion and right action. We have explored together the spiritual significance of the Solstices and of Christmas. We try to answer their questions and encourage them to find answers to some of those questions themselves. Yet, until recently there has been something missing. Our family had no daily ritual. We try to say a blessing or read a special passage before dinner but, often in our busyness, we forget. What could I do with my children every day that would have meaning for all of us?

One day in early autumn the answer simply came to me. It arrived whole in the phrase, "Wish for the World." OK, but how? How could this idea become a ritual, powerful to me, yet accessible to my children?

Over the years I have learned, and frequently practiced, visualization as a tool for discovering my dreams and intentions and unleashing them into the universe. Tibetan Buddhism, through various visual meditations, emphasizes the power of concentrating our minds and intentions upon that which we wish to manifest, most particularly to ease the suffering of all beings. Wicca, too, teaches that to focus our attention is to raise personal power. Growing up I learned to say my prayers. Each night, in my snug bed, I repeated a verse familiar to many of us.

"Now I lay me down to sleep. I pray the Lord my soul to keep. If I should die before I wake, I pray the Lord my soul to take." I also asked that God focus his attention on keeping safe those I loved; my parents and siblings, my friends, my pets. It helped me to feel safe, secure and embraced by something strong and sure. Could I possibly combine these diverse practices into a single cohesive one? Indeed I could.

So now each night, faithfully, we gather in the twin's bedroom and take turns choosing a wish for the world. Sometimes the wish springs immediately to mind. Other times it takes a bit of pondering. They cover such areas of concern as the environment, the earth's creatures, war, disease, famine and genocide. The wishes are simple, direct and powerful. After we wish we all try to focus intently on the wish while I rub Dyson and Ethan's backs and hum the Brahms Lullaby. Sadie and I then go off to her room and repeat the ritual.

My children love it. Sadie snuggles on my lap. Dyson never fails to remind us to wish. Ethan keeps track of whose turn it is to choose the wish. It feels powerful to all of us. We think outside ourselves. We search for ways to better ourselves. We ask for help. We wish for the healing of the world.

I began to imagine the power that we could generate if our small circle could be united with others. What if people all over the world shared the same wish for the world every day? What kind of energy, spiritual and personal, could we all raise together? I believe the potential is enormous and endless. Thus has this book come into being.

I believe in the power of seeing our dreams in our imaginations as we wish for them. When I wish for the world, I create an image of that wish in my mind's eye. To take an example from the book, "We wish for an end to poverty," I visualize people, all over the world, adequately fed, clothed, and housed. I see them going about their daily business with an air of comfort and contentment. I might also imagine people helping others by serving them food, or teaching them skills with which they can support themselves and their families. I remind my children to focus similarly on their own images of the wish. If they have trouble doing that, I help them. We explore together how a world without poverty might look. How we, and others, might help bring that about.

What follows are three hundred and sixty-five wishes for the world created with the help of my two sons. Those based on wishes created by Ethan and Dyson are more childlike. The ones I have composed are a bit more adult in their focus. Throughout I have tried to make them accessible to adults and children alike. I have chosen related inspirational quotations to accompany each wish. These may be used to enhance your vision of the wish. You can also use them as a jumping off point for further conversations about the significance or importance of each wish to the planet and to humanity.

I have described how we wish for the world. I invite you to use our method if it works for you. If not, feel free to adapt it. If the wording bothers you, change it. Should it suit you to begin with a salutation to God, the Buddha or Muhammad, please do. If you choose, you could simply meditate upon the wish in silence. You may already have a daily prayer or meditation practice. If you do, just add the wish for the world at any appropriate moment. All we ask is that you join us. Pick a time each day, and "Wish for the World."

Tonight, as we begin the new year,
our wish is for all people
to have compassion for the suffering
of all beings.

"Every morning, when we wake up, we have
twenty-four brand new hours to live.
What a precious gift! We have the capacity
to live in a way that these twenty-four hours
will bring peace, joy and happiness to ourselves
and others."

—Thich Nhat Hanh,
Peace Is Every Step

2

Our wish for the world tonight
is that there will be
an end to war.

"...the waste of moments sleeping
the waste of pleasure weeping
by denying and ignoring
the waste of nations warring"

—Robert Frost, *November*

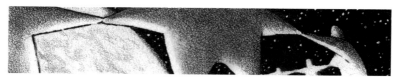

3

Tonight we wish for all people
to be willing to acknowledge
their strengths and
admit their weaknesses.

"To understand yourself
is the beginning of wisdom."

—J. Krishnamurti,
Freedom from the Known

We wish that all nations
will pay greater attention
to cleaning up and stopping
the pollution of our oceans.

"Sunlight pouring into plants, ingested into
the bodies of fish, into the red-winged blackbird,
into the bacteria, into the fungi, into the earth itself.
Because we know ourselves to be made of this earth,
because we know sunlight moves through us,
water moves through us, everything moves,
everything changes, and the daughters
are returned to their mothers."

—Susan Griffin, *Woman and Nature*

5

We wish that people
will stop hurting one another.

"I ask you, presence immanent in all things
to let my fortitude transcend my fear
and bring innate, dispassionate love to bear
on my constricted soul, with healing wings."

—Nessa Rapoport, *Against the Fear of Dying*

6

Tonight we wish for all people,
including ourselves,
to better care for the poor.

"Consequently, the modern poor are not pitied . . .
but written off as trash. The twentieth-century
consumer economy has produced the first culture for
which a beggar is a reminder of nothing."

—John Berger, *In Keeping a Rendezvous*

7

*Our wish for the world tonight
is for an end to poverty.*

"Poverty on a personal and world-wide level
is supported by our mass consciousness belief
in scarcity."

—Shakti Gawain, *Living in the Light*

We wish for the world
that people will learn
to better respect all creatures.

"The tigress and her cubs, who received the flesh
of Mahasattva's body, were reborn, it is said,
as the Buddha's first five disciples,
the very first to receive his teaching
after his enlightenment."

—Sogyal Rinpoche,
The Tibetan Book of Living and Dying

9

We wish for parents
to try harder
not to make their children cry.

"Be patient with children ...
you are dealing with souls."

—Anonymous

10

Tonight our wish for the world
is for each of us to see the world
anew in every moment of every day.

"...whenever you see something important,
you can see it from another perspective if you
step out of the ordinary and look again.
When you see from an extraordinary perspective,
you will know there is spirit in everything."

—Carl A. Hammerschlag, M.D.,
The Theft of the Spirit

We wish that we will live peaceably
with one another and
model peace for our children.

"If we would heal the body, we must first
imagine it well. If we would heal the planet,
we must first envision peace,
not as an abstract wish but as a practical reality..."

—Vicki Noble, *Motherpeace*

Our wish for the world tonight
is that human beings will no longer
kill animals just for fun.

"O you misunderstand, a game is not a law,
this dance is not a whim, this kill is not a rival.
I crackle through your pastures,
I make no profit/like the sun
I burn and burn, this tongue licks through
your body also"

—Margaret Atwood, *Song of the Fox*

JANUARY

13

Tonight we wish that all people
will gaze at eagles.

"To allow ourselves to be truly in touch with
where we already are, no matter where that is,
we have got to pause in our experience long enough
to let the present moment sink in;
long enough to actually *feel* the present moment,
to see it in its fullness..."

—Jon Kabat-Zinn,
Wherever You Go There You Are

Tonight we wish for all people
to reconnect with a community
of Faith and Spirit.

"Brother Warrior, there are none of us
who walk this path alone.
Spirit Healer, it's the only life
that we have ever known....
At this time when the earth is waking
to the dawn of another age,
I tell you now there is no reason to be afraid."

—Kate Wolf, *Brother Warrior*

Our wish for the world tonight is for all people to take good care of their pets.

"I will be your cat, he said to himself, ... if you will be
my housekeepers. And of course they agreed,
because of the white tip of his tail,
because he hummed such a variety of purrs and songs,
because he really was quite a handsome fellow,
and because they had very soft hearts."

—May Sarton, *The Fur Person*

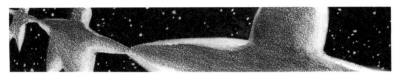

Tonight we wish that we will find
a cure for AIDS.

"My dearest friends despise me;
I have lost everyone I love.
Have pity on me, my friends,
for God's fist has struck me.
Why must you hunt me as God does?
Why do you gnaw my flesh?

—*The Book of Job*,
translated by Stephen Mitchell

17

Tonight our wish for the world
is for human beings
to stop hunting whales.

"The indescribable blend of grace, power, and beauty
of a whale as it glides underwater, leaps toward
the sky, or simply lifts its flukes and slides into the sea
symbolizes a vanishing poetry of the wild."

—Dr. James Darling, *With the Whales*

Tonight we wish for the health of all forests and we remember that all creatures breathe together.

"The truth is that everything contains everything else. We cannot just be, we can only inter-be."

—Thich Nhat Hanh, *Peace Is Every Step*

19

Tonight we wish
that people of all religions
will respect each other.

"Yet there is one significant source of hope
in this tragic situation, and that is
that the spiritual teachings
of all the great mystical traditions
are still available."

—Sogyal Rinpoche,
The Tibetan Book of Living and Dying

Our wish for the world tonight
is for all people to have
enough money to live.

"But if God so clothes the grass of the field,
which is alive today and tomorrow
is thrown into the oven,
will he not much more clothe you?"

—Matthew 23:30, *The Holy Bible*
Revised Standard Version

21

Our wish for the world tonight
is that everyone around the world
will forgive someone.

"Forgiveness is the answer to the child's dream
of a miracle by which what is broken
is made whole again, what is soiled
is made clean again."

—Dag Hammarskjold, *Markings*

22

We wish for
an end to homelessness.

"We can't help everyone,
but everyone can help someone."

—Dr. Loretta Scott

23

We wish for all people
to walk lightly upon the earth.

"The creating power continued:
'Now, if you have learned how to behave
like human beings and how to live in peace
with each other and with the other living things—
the two-legged, the four-legged, the many-legged,
the fliers, the no-legs, the green plants
of this universe, then all will be well.'"

—Told by Leonard Crow Dog,
American Indian Myths and Legends

24

Our wish for the world tonight
is for people with power
to stop forcing others
to do things they do not want to do.

"Leadership is the act of getting someone else
to do something you want done
because he wants to do it."

—Dwight D. Eisenhower

We wish that a lasting peace
will be made in the Middle East.

"If we have no peace, it is because we have
forgotten we belong to each other."

—Mother Theresa

*Our wish for the world tonight
is for all of us to slow down.*

"I'd choose to be a daisy,
If I might be a flower,
Closing my petals softly
At the twilight's quiet hour;
And waking in the morning,
When falls the early dew,
To welcome Heaven's bright sunshine,
And Heaven's bright teardrops, too."

—Author Unknown, *I'd Choose to Be a Daisy*

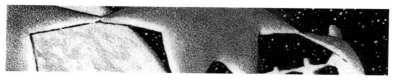

27

Tonight we wish that
we all might listen to the elders.

"To you, O men, I call,
and my cry is to the sons of men.
O simple ones, learn prudence; O foolish men,
pay attention. Hear, for I will speak noble things,
and from my lips will come what is right..."

—Proverbs 8:4–6, *The Holy Bible*
Revised Standard Version

28

*Our wish tonight
is that we may all be courageous.*

"This was not very comforting to Piglet, because
however many pieces of string they tried
pulling up with, it would always be the same him
coming down; but still, it did seem
the only thing to do. So with one last look back
in his mind at all the happy hours he had spent
in the Forest *not* being pulled up to the ceiling
by a piece of string, Piglet nodded bravely at Pooh..."

—A.A. Milne, *The House at Pooh Corner*

We wish to better understand
the intelligence of all creatures.

"Pretty soon this old man had five or six snakes
crawling over his body, raising their heads to look at
his closed eyes and peaceful face, then going to sleep.
It showed they had found their friend, looking
with in this one upon whose body they chose
to rest." (Koahwyma)

—Frank Waters, *Book of the Hopi*

30

Tonight our wish for the world
is for all parents
to hug their children often.

"Children enter the world with a great deal of love
and trust. They are not yet able to perceive good
and bad, but take everything as good and
appropriate to absorb and unconsciously imitate."

—Rahima Baldwin Dancy,
You are Your Child's First Teacher

31

We wish for the world
that more people
will focus on one thing at a time.

"One thing at a time. That's all we have to do.
Not two things at once,
but one thing done in peace."

—Melody Beattie,
The Language of Letting Go

1

We wish to learn to listen well.

"If you study something, listen to something or
are trying to understand something,
you have to do it with a free mind.
If you go on with your own thoughts
at the same time, your mind
will never be free to follow."

—Peter Ouspensky,
The Fourth Way

2

We wish for the world tonight
that all people will cultivate
their ability to be still.

"A man does not seek to see himself in running water,
but in still water. For only what is still itself
can impart stillness to others."

—Chuang Tzu, *Inner Chapters*

3

Tonight we wish for all of us
to overcome our prejudice.

"In moments of self-remembering, there is no time,
nor fear, nor doubt—only pure consciousness,
silence and the voice of conscience."

—Rodney Collin,
The Theory of Conscious Harmony

4

We wish for all people
to pay attention.

"The faculty of bringing back a wandering attention
over and over again
is the very root of judgement..."

—William James,
The Principles of Psychology

5

Tonight we wish for everyone
to comfort each other.

"From looking at your neighbor and realizing
his true significance, and that he will die,
pity and compassion will arise in you for him,
and finally you will love him."

—G.I. Gurdjieff

6

Our wish tonight is for all of us to expand our horizons.

"To see a world in a grain of sand
And Heaven in a Wildflower,
Hold infinity in the palm of your hand,
And eternity in an hour"

—William Blake, *Auguries of Innocence*

7

We wish to see more clearly.

"It is a great art to look at something,
to look at something the way
an innocent child does."

—Jean Klein,
Be Who You Are

8

Our wish for the world tonight
is for ourselves and others
to learn self-discipline.

"If the heart wanders or is distracted, bring it back
to the point quite gently and replace it tenderly
in its master's presence. And even if you did nothing
during the whole hour but bring your heart back
and place it again in our Lord's presence,
though it went away every time you brought it back,
your hour would be very well employed."

—Saint Francis de Sales

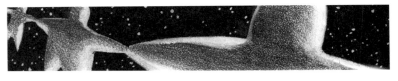

9

Tonight we wish
for a cure for cancer.

"Well, imagine that a miracle occurs one day.
You awake and your skin is completely healed.
There are no wounds anymore,
and it doesn't hurt to be touched."

—Don Miguel Ruiz,
The Mastery of Love

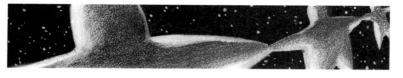

10

We wish for all people
to strive to love unconditionally.

"Pure love has no parallel in power,
and there is no darkness it cannot dispel."

—Meher Baba, *Discourses*

11

Tonight we wish for every child
around the world
to have at least one parent.

"The best way to prepare our children for the stresses
of today's world is not to expose them to problems
early in their life, but to provide them with
an environment that is warm and nurturing and
that shelters them when they are young from as many
of the problems of the adult world as possible."

—Rahima Baldwin Dancy,
You Are Your Child's First Teacher

12

*Our wish for the world tonight
is for all people to learn
to express our anger appropriately.*

"Breathing in, I know that anger is here.
Breathing out, I know that anger is me.
Breathing in, I know that anger is unpleasant.
Breathing out, I know this feeling will pass.
Breathing in, I am calm.
Breathing out, I am strong enough
to take care of this anger."

—Thich Nhat Hanh,
Peace Is Every Step

13

Tonight we wish
that all adults will mirror tolerance
for our children and others.

"I am not a 'statesman in the garb of a saint.'
But since Truth is the highest wisdom,
sometimes my acts appear to be consistent
with the highest statesmanship.
But I hope I have no policy in me
save the policy of Truth and Non-violence..."

—M.K. Gandhi,
The Essential Gandhi

14

Our wish for the world tonight
is that all people will stop smoking.

"You must do the thing
you think you cannot do."

—Eleanor Roosevelt

15

Our wish for the world tonight
is to stop polluting
the world's oceans.

"All things come from the Goddess
and to her they shall return.
Like a drop of rain
flowing to the ocean."

—Wicca chant, author unknown

16

We wish that all those who hunt
will use all they take.

"While the Craft recognizes that life feeds on life
and that we must kill in order to survive,
life is never taken needlessly,
never squandered or wasted."

—Starhawk, *The Spiral Dance*

17

Tonight we wish
for people to respect fire.

"Of all the early techniques, fire was the most
powerful and versatile: it allowed people to
turn grain into bread, clay into stone,
inflammable matter to ashes."

—Vicki Noble, *Motherpeace*

18

We wish tonight
that all who suffer from depression
will find relief.

"Through many dangers, toils and snares,
I have already come;
'Tis grace hath brought me safe thus far,
and grace will lead me home."

—John Newton, *Amazing Grace*

19

Our wish tonight is for all of us
to work harder to develop and use
renewable resources.

"A civilization flourishes when people
plant trees under which
they will never sit."

—Greek Proverb

20

Tonight we wish for the world
that human beings will respect
the spirits of all creatures.

"All things bright and beautiful,
All creatures great and small,
All things wise and wonderful,
The Lord God made them all."

—Cecil Frances Alexander,
All Things Bright and Beautiful

21

We wish to do more
to clean up our waterways.

"The great sea has set me in motion.
Set me adrift,
And I move as a weed in the river.
The arch of sky
And mightiness of storms
Encompass me,
And I am left
Trembling with joy."

—Eskimo song

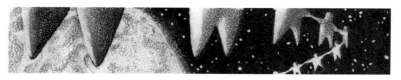

22

Tonight we wish for the world
that people will stop littering.

"How far must suffering and misery go before
we see that even in the day of vast cities
and powerful machines, the good earth is
our mother and that if we destroy her,
we destroy ourselves?"

—Paul Bigelow Sears

23

We wish tonight
to be more generous.

"How wonderful that no one need wait
a single moment to improve the world."

—Anne Frank

24

Our wish for the world
is for all people
to strive for compassion.

"Out of compassion I destroy the darkness
of their ignorance. From within them
I light the lamp of wisdom and dispel
all darkness from their lives."

—Bhagavad Gita

25

We wish to do less
to pollute our air.

"It is by acts and not by ideas
that people live."

—Anatole France

26

*Our wish for the world tonight
is for all of us to be kind to those
who are different from us.*

"The greatest discovery of any generation is that
human beings can alter their lives by altering
the attitudes of their minds."

—Albert Schweitzer

27

Tonight we wish that all people will spay and neuter their pets.

"The greatness of a nation and its moral progress
can be judged by the way
its animals are treated."

—M.K. Gandhi

28

*Our wish for the world tonight
is for all children to have homes.*

"I have one last thing I want the world to know about
homelessness. It is that it is not the person's fault.
It is not a choice—it just comes and if we work
together, we can overcome homelessness."

—Shoniqua Williams, age 11

29

We wish for everyone
to dance freely sometimes.

"We need to dance with life.
Swim in the Soul of your eyes.
'Till we melt into the night.
O, we need to dance with life,
And leave a brilliant light behind...."

—Bernie Taupin and Martin Page,
Dance with Life

Tonight we wish for everyone
to have enough food.

"The earth is a generous mother; she will provide
in plentiful abundance food for all her children
if they will but cultivate her soil in justice
and in peace."

—Bourke Coekran

Tonight we wish
to forgive ourselves.

"Once you have experienced and released
blocked emotions from the past,
a greater flow of energy and vitality
will enrich your life."

—Shakti Gawain,
Living in the Light

Our wish for the world tonight
is that everyone learns to read.

"Beyond the formative effects of reading
on the individuals composing society, the fact that
they have read the same books gives them
experiences and ideas in common....
That is what we mean when we say figuratively
of another person, 'We speak the same language.'"

—Charles Scribner, Jr.,
Publishers Weekly

Our wish for the world tonight
is that everyone has
clean clothes to wear.

"This mournful truth is everywhere confess'd—
Slow rises worth by poverty depress'd"

—Samuel Johnson

We wish tonight
to be facilitators of peace.

"Mankind must remember that peace is not
God's gift to his creatures;
peace is our gift to each other."

—Elie Wiesel

6

Tonight we wish that all people
will care for the elders in their lives.

―――――――――――

"A test of a people is how it behaves toward the old.
It is easy to love children. Even tyrants and dictators
make a point of being fond of children.
But the affection and care for the old,
the incurable, the helpless
are the true gold mines of a culture."

—Abraham Heschel

Tonight we wish to overcome hatred
all over the world.

"As I have said, the first thing is to be honest
with yourself. You can never have an impact
on society if you have not changed yourself....
Great peacemakers are all people of integrity,
of honesty, but humility."

—Nelson Mandela

8

Our wish for the world tonight
is for everyone to learn how
to breathe more deeply.

"Live in each season as it passes;
breathe the air, drink the drink,
taste the fruit, and resign yourself
to the influences of each."

—Henry David Thoreau, *Journals*

Tonight we wish for an end
to child abuse.

"Child abuse casts a shadow
the length of a lifetime."

—Herbert Ward

We wish for everyone
to make an effort
to preserve all species of life.

"Life forms illogical patterns. It is haphazard and
full of beauties which I try to catch as they fly by,
for who knows whether any of them
will every return."

—Margo Fonteyn

*Our wish for the world tonight
is for more people to teach equality.*

"The power of a movement lies in the fact that
it can indeed change the habits of people.
This change is not the result of force
but of dedication, of moral persuasion."

—Stephen Biko

12

Tonight we wish for people
all around the world
to be able to see.

"Man is a sun and his senses
are his planets."

—Novalis

MARCH

13

We wish that everyone
gets to see new places.

"The real meaning of travel, like that of
a conversation by the fireside, is the discovery
of oneself through contact with other people."

—Paul Tournier,
The Meaning of Persons

14

Our wish for the world tonight
is for everyone to sleep
deeply and well.

"Rocked in the cradle of the deep.
I lay me down in peace to sleep."

—Emma Willard,
The Cradle of the Deep

We wish tonight that all people will have clean drinking water.

"Water, water, everywhere,
nor any drop to drink."

—Samuel Taylor Coleridge,
The Ancient Mariner

16

*Our wish for the world tonight
is for everyone to be able
to climb a mountain.*

"I believe in an extraconciousness that
looks after you. It only comes into play
in extreme circumstances, which for me
is in the mountains."

—Roger Marshall

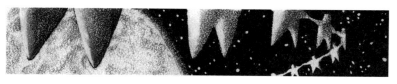

MARCH

17

We wish that parents
will listen to their children.

"I have found the best way to give advice
to your children is to find out what they want
and then advise them to do it."

—Harry S. Truman

Tonight we wish
to strive to heal ourselves.

"What can we gain by sailing to the moon
if we are not able to cross the abyss
that separates us from ourselves?
This is the most important of all voyages of discovery,
and without it, all the rest are not only useless,
but disastrous."

—Thomas Merton

Our wish for the world tonight is for all of us to take good care of our bodies.

"You *are* your body. The body that you can see and touch is only a thin illusory veil. Underneath it lies the invisible inner body, the doorway into Being, into Life Unmanifested. Through the inner body you are inseparably connected to this unmanifested One Life— birthless, deathless, eternally present"

—Eckhart Tolle, *The Power of Now*

We wish tonight that everyone
will have something or someone
to care for.

"Too often we underestimate the power of a touch,
a smile, a kind word, a listening ear, an honest
compliment, or the smallest act of caring,
all of which have the potential
to turn a life around."

—Leo Buscaglia

21

Tonight we wish that everyone
who needs a job finds one.

"Work and love—these are the basics.
Without them there is neurosis."

—Theodore Reik,
Of Love and Lust

Tonight we wish for everyone
to have the chance
to go to the beach.

"Those who contemplate the beauty of the earth
find reserves of strength that will endure
as long as life lasts."

—Rachel Carlson

Our wish for the world tonight
is for all people to nurture
their chosen form of spirituality.

"Naturally, we cannot say much about the spiritual
body, because we cannot imagine what it would be
like to have a spiritual body different from that
which we now inhabit, but it seems to me
reasonable to believe that we are
weaving our spiritual bodies
as we go along"

—W.R. Mathews

We wish for everyone
to have time to play.

"Play is the exultation of the possible."

—Martin Buber

Tonight we wish that everyone
has lots of books on their beds.

"I still find each day too short for all the thoughts
I want to think, all the walks I want to take,
all the books I want to read, and all
the friends I want to see."

—John Borrough

MARCH
26

Our wish for the world tonight
is for everyone around the world
to have at least one warm thing.

"They were out of the snow now, but it was very cold,
and to keep warm they sang a song right through
six times, Piglet doing the tiddely-poms and
Pooh doing the rest of it. And in a little while
they felt much warmer, and were able
to talk again."

—A.A. Milne,
The House at Pooh Corner

Tonight we wish
that we all get to meet new people.

"A sound arises out of the earth ...
a singing, a friendliness."

—Adric Wright

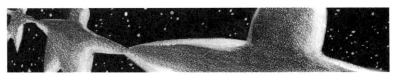

We wish tonight for everyone
to get enough rest.

"...We want to rest. We need to rest and allow
the earth to rest. We need to reflect and
to rediscover the mystery that lives in us,
that is the ground of every unique expression
of life, the source of the fascination that
calls all things to communion."

—U.N. Environmental Sabbath Program

Our wish for the world tonight
is that everyone learns to write.

"No nation ancient or modern ever lost the liberty of
freely speaking, writing or publishing their sentiments
but forthwith lost their liberty in general
and became slaves."

—John Peter Zanger

We wish for an alleviation
of suffering in Africa.

"During my lifetime I have dedicated myself
to this struggle of the African people,
I have fought against white domination, and
I have fought against black domination.
I have cherished the ideal of a democratic and free
society in which all persons live together in harmony
and with equal opportunities. It is an ideal which I
hope to live for and to achieve. But if it needs be
it is an ideal for which I am prepared to die"

—Nelson Mandela

Tonight we wish that
we would all smile at everyone
with whom we interact each day.

"Step onto the Planet.
Draw a circle a hundred feet around.
Inside the circle are
300 things nobody understands, and maybe
nobody's ever really seen.
How many can you find?"

—Lew Welch

We wish to be
compassionate supporters
of those we love.

"The friend who can be silent with us in a moment
of despair or confusion, who can stay with us
in an hour of grief and bereavement, who can
tolerate not knowing, not curing, not healing
and face with us the reality of our powerlessness,
that is a friend who cares."

—Henri Nouwen, *Out of Solitude*

Tonight we wish for ourselves
and others to try
not to be afraid of things
that are not real.

"From within the light all the spontaneous sounds
of the dharma will come like the roar of a thousand
thunder claps.... Do not be afraid of it, do not escape,
do not fear. Recognize it as the play of our own mind,
your own projection."

—*The Tibetan Book of the Dead*

Our wish for the world tonight
is that people not use drugs
in bad ways.

"I had to take one more tiny blue valium, and then
a Halcion, which is a sleeping pill that they have
banned in most civilized countries because of
unpleasant side effects. For instance,
it makes you feel like killing people."

—Anne LaMott, *Traveling Mercies*

Tonight we wish that
everyone has a chance
to sit on a hill.

"You ask
why I perch
on a jade green mountain?
I laugh
but say nothing
my heart
free
like a peach blossom..."

—Li Po

Our wish for the world
is that all children be able
to go to school.

"A mind once stretched by a new idea
never regains its original dimension."

—Oliver Wendell Holmes

Tonight we wish for all people
to have warm comfortable beds.

"...This day you led us wonderfully. Everybody went
to his mat satisfied and full. Renew us during
our sleep, that in the morning we may
come afresh to our daily jobs."

—Ghanaian Christian Prayer,
Earth Prayers

We wish for suffering
to ease in America.

"To be free of time is to be free of the psychological
need of past for your identity and future
for your fulfillment. It represents the most profound
transformation of consciousness
that you can imagine."

—Eckhart Tolle, *The Power of Now*

APRIL

8

Our wish for the world tonight
is for everyone to teach tolerance.

"The test of courage comes when we are
in the minority. The test of tolerance comes
when we are in the majority."

—Ralph Washington Sockman

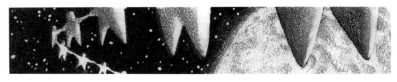

We wish for the dolphins to be saved.

"It is an important and popular fact that things are
not always as they seem. For instance,
on the planet Earth, man had always assumed that
he was more intelligent than dolphins because
he had achieved so much—the wheel, New York,
wars and so on—whilst all the dolphins had ever done
was muck about in the water having a good time.
But conversely, the dolphins had always believed
that they were far more intelligent then man—
for precisely the same reasons."

—Douglas Adams,
The Hitchhikers Guide to the Galaxy

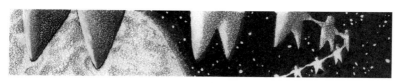

10

Tonight we wish for
an end to sexual abuse.

"We are in pain. The pain is excruciating.
We cannot escape it. We cannot escape.
It hounds us. It tells us we should not exist."

—Susan Griffin, *Woman and Nature*

Our wish for the world is
for parents to stop
neglecting their children.

"Everything proceeds as of its own accord, and this
can all too easily tempt us to relax and let things
take their course without troubling over the details.
Such indifference is the root of all evil."

—I Ching

We wish tonight for all people
to respect everyone.

"Conscience is not the same thing for all.
Whilst, therefore, it is a good guide for individual
conduct, imposition of that conduct upon all
will be an insufferable interference....
Mutual toleration can be inculcated among
and practiced by all, irrespective of
their status and training."

—M.K. Gandhi, *The Essential Ghandi*

We wish for everyone
to work harder at resolving conflicts.

"Most of us want to take sides in each encounter
or conflict. We distinguish right from wrong
based on partial evidence or hearsay.
We need indignation in order to act, but even
righteous, legitimate indignation is not enough....
What we need are people who are capable of loving,
of not taking sides so that they can embrace
the whole of reality."

—Thich Nhat Hanh,
Peace Is Every Step

APRIL

14

Tonight we wish to feel
everything that is ours to feel.

"I feel ecstasy in living;
the mere sense of living is joy enough."

—Emily Dickinson

We wish to approach all life
with reverence every day.

"A man and a woman
Are one.
A man and a woman and a blackbird
Are one..."

—Wallace Stevens,
Thirteen Ways of Looking at a Blackbird

APRIL

16

*Our wish for the world tonight
is that we shall model compassion
for others.*

"How far you go in life depends on your being
tender with the young, compassionate with the aged,
sympathetic with the striving and tolerant of
the weak and the strong. Because someday in life
you will have been all of these."

—George Washington Carver

17

We wish tonight for all people to overcome bigotry.

"We hate what we fear, and where hate is,
fear is lurking."

—Cyril Vernon Connolly

*Our wish for the world tonight
is for everyone, all over the world,
to learn from their elders.*

"The great thing about getting older
is that you don't lose all the other ages
you've been."

—Madeleine L'Engle

Our wish for the world tonight is for everyone to stop worrying so much.

"We are, perhaps, uniquely among the earth's
creatures, the worrying animal. We worry
away our lives, fearing the future,
discontent with the present..."

—Lewis Thomas,
The Medusa and the Snail

We wish for an end to starvation.

"Our marvels of science and technology are matched,
if not outweighed, by many current tragedies
including human starvation in some parts
of the world.... We have the capability
and the responsibility. We must act
before it is too late."

—The Dalai Lama

Tonight we wish for everyone
to do what they can to save the tiger.

"First and foremost: know the following facts
about tigers: Tiger is a thorough gentleman.
Tiger is not a bloodthirsty killer.
Tiger kills only for food and only when hungry.
If Tiger dies we are soon to become extinct
for Tiger is an apex species,
indicator of the health of the forests."

—Uday Patel

We wish tonight
to be grateful for what we have.

"Gratitude unlocks the fullness of life.
It turns what we have into enough, and more...."

—Melody Beattie

APRIL

23

Our wish for the world tonight
is that everyone,
at some point in their lives,
goes into a cave.

"Look deep, deep into nature, and then
you will understand everything better."

—Albert Einstein

APRIL

24

We wish for everyone who is cold
to become warm enough.

"The greatest of our evils and the worst of our crimes
is poverty."

—George Bernard Shaw,
Major Barbara

Tonight we wish that
more animal habitat
will be preserved.

"What is man without the beasts? If all the beasts
were gone, man would die from loneliness of spirit.
For whatever happens to the beasts happens to men.
All things are connected..."

—Chief Seattle

We wish tonight for the ability
to express our love openly.

"This is the miracle that happens every time
to those who really love; the more they give,
the more they possess."

—Rainier Maria Rilke

Our wish for the world tonight
is for all people to listen to bird song
more attentively.

"...While I am lying on the grass
Thy twofold shout I hear;
From hill to hill it seems to pass,
At once far off, and near.
Though babbling only to the Vale
Of sunshine and of flowers,
Though bringest unto me a tale.
Of visionary hours."

—William Wordsworth, *To the Cuckoo*

We wish everyone gets a chance
to play in the snow.

"Your work is to discover your world and then
with all your heart give yourself to it."

—The Buddha

APRIL

29

We wish to eat more slowly
in order to taste our food more fully.

"The ordinary acts we practice every day at home
are of more importance to the soul
than their simplicity might suggest."

—Thomas Moore

Tonight we wish
to not interrupt others
and to not be interrupted.

"Bad habits are like a comfortable bed,
easy to get into, but hard to get out of."

—Anonymous

Our wish for the world tonight
is for people to try not to hit animals
when they are in their boats.

"We call them dumb animals, and so they are,
for they cannot tell us how they feel,
but they do not suffer less
because they have no words."

—Anna Sewell, *Black Beauty*

Tonight we wish to do more
to clean up the earth.

"We have probed the earth, excavated it, burned it,
ripped things from it, buried things in it....
That does not fit my definition of a good tenant.
If we were here on a month-to-month basis,
we would have been evicted long ago."

—Rose Elizabeth Bird

We wish for ourselves and others
to learn to let go.

"So letting go is what the whole game is.
You turn on the lights and
the cockroaches run away.
You can never grasp them."

—John Lennon

We wish tonight for everyone
to teach spirituality to their children.

"He would spend the next forty-five years of his life
tramping tirelessly through the cities
of the Ganges plain, bringing his Damma (Dharma)
to gods, animals, men and women.
There could be no limits to his
compassionate offensive."

—Karen Armstrong, *Buddha*

MAY

5

Our wish for the world tonight
is for all of us to find a way
to acknowledge everyone.

"Whenever I meet people I always approach them
from the standpoint of the most basic things
we have in common ... we are all born
the same way, and we all die...."

—The Dalai Lama,
The Art of Happiness

We wish that
there be no more homeless animals.

"But there are also those who are the outcasts
of society—unwanted, lame, too traumatized
by past abuse, or too old, handicapped or ill.
For these innocent creatures Best Friends
is a unique home and haven."

—Best Friends Animal Sanctuary,
Kanab, Utah

MAY

7

Our wish for the world
is that we all reuse
as much as possible.

"To cherish what remains of the earth and
to foster its renewal is our only
legitimate hope for survival."

—Wendell Berry

Tonight we wish that
people all over the world will
learn to be more patient
with each other.

"Patience is the companion of wisdom."

—St. Augustine, *On Patience*

MAY

9

We wish tonight that couples
will listen to each other
more attentively.

"The first duty of love is to listen."

—Paul Tillich

We wish more people
will ride bikes.

"Where am I going? I don't know.
Down to the stream where the king cups grow—
Up on the hill where the pine trees blow.
Anywhere, anywhere, *I* don't know."

—A. A. Milne, *Spring Morning*

MAY

11

Our wish for the world tonight is for everyone to experience a garden.

"It is *the* moment now. Daffodils, many different kinds, are glorious ... small bright red tulips wonderful also. It is *the* moment because the leaves on the trees have not yet sprung, so the light and sky shine through feathery, just swelling twigs."

—May Sarton, *Journal of a Solitude*

We wish to be able to sit with
our friends when they are sad.

"... in that place when even the purity of silence
was not granted me, solitude turned sour, and
dreams flaunted themselves, skewed, awry;
toward that place where no one dared to visit
lest they, too, succumb, you stretched out your hand
and would not be refused, spoke in natural tones,
mussed, listened without fear to frightful things...."

—Nessa Rapoport,
Letter to a Friend Who Did Not Abandon Me

MAY

13

Tonight we wish that all people
will feel compassion for animals.

"A human being is a part of the whole that we call
the universe, a part limited in time and space.
He experiences himself, his thoughts and feelings,
as something separated from the rest—a kind of
optical illusion of his consciousness.
This illusion is a prison for us....
Our task must be to free ourselves from this prison
by widening our circle of compassion
to embrace all of nature."

—Albert Einstein

MAY

14

Our wish for the world tonight is for all people to respect their children.

"If we could raise one generation
with unconditional love, there would be no Hitlers.
We need to teach the next generation of children
from Day One that they are responsible
for their lives.... We can make our choices
built from love or from fear."

—Elizabeth Kübler-Ross

We wish to be teachers of peace.

"I do not want the peace
which passeth understanding,
I want the understanding
which bringeth peace."

—Helen Keller

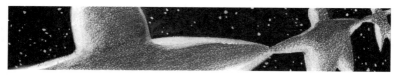

MAY
16

Tonight we wish for an end
to suffering in South America.

"We can not depend on governments
to heal our wounds.
We have to help each other."

—Hene, Maori Woman Elder

Our wish for the world is for an end
to the neglect of our elders.

"Nothing—not avarice, not pride, not scrupulousness,
not impulsiveness—so disillusions a youth
about her parents as the seemingly inhumane way
they treat her grandparents."

—Louise J. Kaplan, *Adolescence*

We wish to always remember
that the earth is alive.

"The earth is at the same time mother,
she is mother of all that is natural,
mother of all that is human.
She is the mother of all, for contained in her
are the seeds of all...."

—Hildegard of Bingen

*Our wish for the world tonight
is to honor the sacred
in all creatures.*

"Apprehend God in all things, for God is in all things.
Every single creature is full of God and is a book
about God. Every creature is a word of God.
If I spent enough time with the tiniest creature—
even a caterpillar—I would never have to
prepare a Sermon. So full of God
is every creature."

—Meister Eckhart

Tonight we wish to be happy about what we do well and not frustrated with what we're not so good at.

"When you have confidence, you can have a lot of fun. And when you have fun, you can do amazing things."

—Joe Namath

We wish for the world that we,
and all people, will practice
what we don't do so well
so that we can learn to do it better.

"If you add a little to a little, and then do it again,
soon that little will be much."

—Hesiod

MAY

22

We wish to always
honor our friends.

"This is the most profound spiritual truth I know:
that even when we're most sure that love
can't conquer all, it seems to anyway. It goes down
into the rat hole with us, in the guise of our friends,
and there it swells and comforts. It gives us
second winds, third winds,
hundredth winds."

—Anne Lamott,
Traveling Mercies

Our wish is for ourselves and others
to be more thoughtful.

"Never doubt that a small group of thoughtful,
committed citizens can change the world.
Indeed, it is the only thing that ever has."

—Margaret Mead

MAY
24

We wish tonight that everyone
will drive their cars more carefully.

"Sometimes when I consider what tremendous
consequences come from little things,
I am tempted to think there are no little things."

—Bruce Barton

MAY

25

Our wish for the world tonight
is that more people use
natural alternatives to pesticides
in their gardens.

"Don't spit in the well.
You might want to drink from it."

—Scottish Proverb

Tonight we wish to learn to
face death openly.

"This existence of ours is as transient
as autumn clouds. To watch the birth and death
of beings is like looking at the movements of a dance.
A lifetime is a flash of lightening in the sky,
rushing by, like a torrent down a steep mountain."

—The Buddha

*Our wish for the world
is for all people to walk attentively.*

"Although we walk all the time, our walking is usually
more like running. When we walk like that,
we print anxiety and sorrow on the earth.
We have to walk in a way that we only
print peace and serenity on the earth."

—Thich Nhat Hahn,
Peace Is Every Step

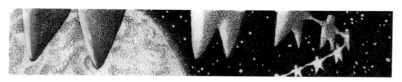

Tonight we wish to listen better
to our inner voice of wisdom.

"the truth of the matter is that you always know
the right thing to do. The hard part is doing it."

—H. Norman Schwarzkopf

MAY

29

We wish for the world that people will ask more questions.

"The important thing is not to stop questioning.
Curiosity has its own reason for existing.
One cannot help but be in awe when
he contemplates the mysteries of eternity,
of life, of the marvelous structure of reality....
Never lose a holy curiosity."

—Albert Einstein

We wish to always
be good neighbors.

"I want you to be concerned about
your next door neighbors.
Do you know your next door neighbor?"

—Mother Teresa

Tonight we wish for society
to better support divorced families.

"Divorce is not something you do and it's over.
You live divorce for the rest of your life, unless you
were married for a short period and had no children.
Divorce is a label you wear, and in this society,
a handicap until we prove it otherwise."

—Constance Ahrons, Ph.D., *The Good Divorce*

We wish for all people to fight slavery
in the places it still exists
around the world.

"Slavery was the first human rights issue
to arouse wide international concern.
Yet, in the face of universal condemnation,
slavery-like practices remain a grave
and persistent problem...."

—United Nations High Commissioner
for Human Rights

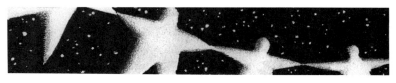

Our wish for the world
is for everyone to experience
a tunnel.

"The most beautiful thing we can experience
is the mysterious. It is the source of all true art
and science. He to whom this emotion is a stranger,
who can no longer pause to wonder and
stand rapt in awe is as good as dead...."

—Albert Einstein

3

Tonight we wish for
an end to the destruction
of the world's coral reefs.

"Coral reefs are suffering globally.
Scientists report that thirty percent of them
are already damaged."

—Reef Relief

We wish tonight
to cultivate our equanimity.

"Loving-kindness, compassion, sympathetic joy, and
equanimity are the four highest emotions,
the only ones worth having. They bring us
to a level on which life gains breadth, greatness,
and beauty and on which we stop trying
to make it run the way we want it to—
on which we even learn to love something
that we may not have wanted at all."

—Ayya Khema,
The Four Highest Emotions

*Our wish for the world tonight
is for everyone to laugh out loud.*

"You can turn painful situations around
through laughter. If you can find humor in anything—
even poverty—you can survive it."

—Bill Cosby

JUNE
6

We wish that everyone
will use only what they need.

"Teach your children what we have taught
our children—that the earth is our mother.
Whatever befalls the earth befalls the sons
and daughters of earth. If men spit upon the ground,
they spit upon themselves."

—Chief Seattle

Tonight we wish
that drivers will try harder
not to run over animals
with their cars.

"I hear a voice,
the cry of a wounded animal;
Someone shoots an arrow at the moon;
A small bird has fallen from the nest.
Witness must be given,
So that life can be guarded."

—W.S. Rendra

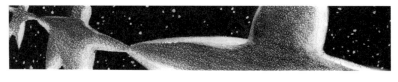

JUNE
8

We wish tonight for everyone
to honor the earth's seasons.

"Again, again we come and go, changed, changing.
Hands join, union in love and fear, grief and joy.
The circles turn, each giving into each, into all."

—Wendell Berry

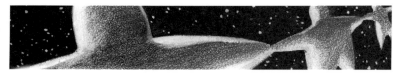

Our wish for the world tonight
is to pay attention to our parents.

"I talk and talk and talk, and I haven't taught people
in fifty years what my father taught me
by example in one week."

—Mario Cuomo

*Our wish is
to be good sounding boards.*

"Great opportunities to help others seldom come,
but small ones surround us every day."

—Sally Koch

Our wish is for everyone
to have time to explore.

"'We're going to discover the North Pole.'
'Oh!' said Pooh again. 'What *is* the North Pole?'
he asked. 'It's just a thing you discover,'
said Christopher Robin carelessly,
not being quite sure himself."

—A.A. Milne, *Winnie the Pooh*

We wish tonight for everyone
to continue to learn new things.

"Only the curious will learn and only the resolute
overcome the obstacles to learning.
The quest quotient has always excited me
more than the intelligence quotient."

—Eugene S. Wilson

13

Tonight we wish for everyone
to have fun.

"A happy person is not a person in a certain set
of circumstances, but rather a person
with a certain set of attitudes."

—Hugh Downs

JUNE

14

Our wish for the world is for
everyone to have the opportunity
to grow vegetables.

"Be a gardener. Dig a ditch, toil and sweat, and
turn the earth upside down and seek the deepness
and water the plants in time. Continue this
labor and make sweet floods to run and
noble and abundant fruits to spring.
Take this food and drink and
carry it to God as your true worship."

—Julian of Norwich

Tonight we wish for all people
to be more mindful.

"The fact that I am standing there and
washing these bowls is a wondrous reality.
I'm being completely myself, following my breath,
conscious of my presence and conscious of
my thoughts and actions."

—Thich Nhat Hahn,
The Miracle of Mindfulness

JUNE
16

We wish to respect our friends.

"Respect your fellow human beings, treat them fairly,
disagree with them honestly, enjoy their friendship,
explore your thoughts with one another candidly,
work together for a common goal and
help one another achieve it."

—Bill Bradley

Our wish for the world tonight is for all people to appreciate their joy.

"To be able to find joy in another's joy:
that is the secret of happiness."

—George Bernanos

Tonight we wish for everyone
to be able to ask for help
when they need it.

"I claim to be a simple individual liable to err
like any other fellow mortal. I own, however,
that I have humility enough to confess my errors
and to retrace my steps."

—M. K. Gandhi

We wish tonight for people
all around the world
to get the chance to puddle jump.

"Keeping in touch with childhood memories
keeps us believing in life's simplest pleasures
like a rainy afternoon, a swingset, and
a giant puddle to play in."

—Chrissy Ogden

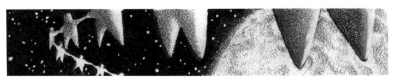

We wish to save the Asian elephants.

"The Asian elephant's numbers are decreasing mainly
because of habitat loss. It's natural home is in
the tropical forest of India and Asia, but much
of this area has been cleared for farmers
to plant crops. Many elephants then move
to the open plains, where they are
easy targets for hunters and traders."

—Thinkquest.org Library

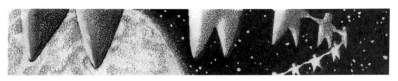

Our wish for the world tonight
is for all of us to notice and
appreciate our changes.

"The garden is growth and change and that means
loss as well as constant new treasures
to make up for a few disasters."

—May Sarton

We wish for each of us
to find our own ways to pray.

"...We must pray for strength. We must pray
to come together, Pray to the weeping earth,
pray to the trembling waters and to
the wandering rain. We must pray to
the whispering moon, pray to the tip-toeing stars
and to the hollering sun."

—Nancy Wood

Tonight we wish for
the safe removal of landmines
worldwide.

"Land-mines are uniquely savage in the history
of modern conventional warfare not only because of
their appalling individual impact, but also
their long term social and economic destruction."

—Graça Machel, United Nations

*Our wish for the world tonight
is for everyone to have time
to play in the rain.*

"John had
Great Big
Waterproof
Boots on;
John had a
Great Big
Waterproof
Hat;
John had a Great Big
Waterproof Mackintosh—
And that
(Said John)
Is
That"

—A.A. Milne, *Happiness*

We wish tonight
to find some small way
to help someone every day.

"I believe that every human mind feels pleasure
in doing good to another."

—Thomas Jefferson

Tonight we wish to learn how to prevent children from killing other children.

"He was the kind of kid whose father owned guns and didn't keep his son from getting to them. The kind of kid who was picked on, often, at his large suburban school. The kind of kid who spent a weekend telling his closest friends— and their parents—that he was going to go to school on Monday and shoot as many of his classmates as he could."

—Meredith Maran,
Deadly Ambivalence

JUNE

27

We wish for all of us
to question ourselves.

"In the attitude of silence the soul finds the path
in clearer light, and what is elusive and deceptive
resolves itself into crystal clearness.
Our life is a long and arduous quest
after the truth."

—M. K. Gandhi

Our wish tonight is for more people
to use natural alternatives
to chemical fertilizers.

"I have come to terms with the future.
From this day onward I will walk easy on the earth.
Plant trees. Kill no living things. Live in harmony
with all creatures. I will restore the earth where I am.
Use no more of its resources than I need.
And listen, listen to what it is telling me."

—M.J. Slim Hooey

We wish for each of us
to always be a good friend.

"I believe that unarmed truth and unconditional love
will have the final word in reality."

—Martin Luther King, Jr.

JUNE

30

We wish tonight for everyone
to be able to dig in the dirt.

"If a healthy soil is full of death, it is also full of life:
worms, fungi, microorganisms of all kinds....
Given only the health of the soil,
nothing that dies is dead for long."

—Wendell Berry,
The Unsettling of America

Our wish for the world tonight
is for the preservation
of all creatures.

"Every creature is better alive than dead,
men and moose and pine trees, and he
who understands it aright will rather
preserve its life than destroy it."

—Henry David Thoreau,
The Maine Woods

JULY

2

Tonight we wish for an end
to poverty in Pakistan.

"What a devil art thou, Poverty! How many desires—
how many aspirations after goodness and truth—
how many noble thoughts, loving wishes
toward our fellows, beautiful imaginings thou hast
crushed under thy heel, without remorse or pause!"

—Walt Whitman

We wish to pay greater attention
to our own life cycles.

"Every day is a little life: every waking and rising
a little birth, every fresh morning a little youth,
every going to rest and sleep a little death."

—Arthur Schopenhauer,
Counsels and Maxims

Tonight we wish that everyone knows
it is alright to cry out loud.

"Pain and suffering are always inevitable for
a large intelligence and a deep heart.
The really great man must, I think,
have great sadness on earth."

—Fyodor Dostoyevsky

Our wish for the world tonight
is to help others whenever possible.

"People seldom refuse help,
if one offers it in the right way."

—A. C. Benson

JULY

6

Tonight we wish to for all people
to learn some form of meditation.

"In us, there is a river of feelings, in which every drop
of water is a different feeling, and each feeling relies
on all the others for its existence. To observe it,
we just sit on the bank of the river and identify
each feeling as it surfaces, flows by,
and disappears."

—Thich Nhat Hahn,
Peace Is Every Step

We wish for the liberation of Tibet.

"Openly questioning the way the world works and
challenging the power of the powerful
is not an activity customarily rewarded."

—Dale Spender, *Women of Ideas and
What Men Have Done to Them*

Our wish tonight is for everyone
to truly enjoy the sunshine.

"Self-forgetfulness should be one's goal,
not self-absorption."

—Valrie Solanas,
The Scum Manifesto

JULY

9

We wish tonight for all people
to have an opportunity
to float on a river.

"Nature is trying very hard to make us succeed,
but nature does not depend on us.
We are not the only experiment."

—R. Buckminster Fuller

We wish that people
will not drink and drive.

"In the past decade, four times as many Americans
died in drunk driving crashes as were killed in
the Vietnam War."

—Mothers Against
Drunk Driving, 1995

We wish tonight for happiness
for all people.

"Happiness is a butterfly which when pursued
is always just beyond your grasp, but which,
if you will sit down quietly
may alight upon you."

—Nathaniel Hawthorne

JULY

12

We wish for an end to terrorism
around the world.

"We must learn to live together as brothers
or perish together as fools."

—Martin Luther King, Jr.

Tonight we wish that all people,
particularly Americans,
will use less gasoline.

"We do not inherit this land from our ancestors.
We borrow it from our children."

—Haida Indian Saying

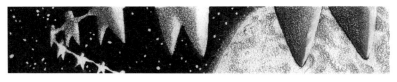

14

Tonight we wish to learn about
other cultures.

"I do desire that we may be better strangers."

William Shakespeare, *As You Like it*.

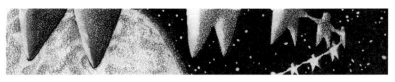

We wish for the world tonight
that all people will pray for the dead.

"Only when you drink from the river of silence
shall you indeed sing. And when you have
reached the mountain top, then you shall
begin to climb. And when the earth
shall claim your limbs,
then shall you truly dance."

—Kahlil Gibran, *The Prophet*

We wish to celebrate birth.

"Just because birth happens everyday
Does not make it ordinary..."

—Anonymous

JULY

17

We wish tonight to remember to say,
"I love you" more often.

"One word frees us of all the weight and pain of life:
That word is love."

—Sophocles

Tonight we wish to seek connection
with others.

"Ideologies separate us. Dreams and anguish
bring us together."

—Eugene Ionesco

We wish tonight to give more
to the charity of our choice.

"Surplus wealth is a sacred trust which its possessor
is bound to administer in his lifetime for
the good of the community."

—Andrew Carnegie

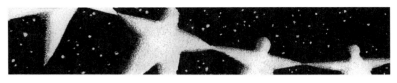

Our wish for the world tonight
is to foster understanding
among nations.

"No man is an island, entire of itself;
every man is a piece of the continent."

—John Donne, *Devotions*

We wish for all people
to search for their
own personal truth.

"It is easier to perceive error than to find truth,
for the former lies on the surface and is easily seen,
while the latter lies in the depth,
where few are willing to search for it."

—Johann Wolfgang von Goethe

Tonight we wish to accept
the personal truth of others.

"The greatest friend of truth is Time,
her greatest enemy is Prejudice, and
her constant companion is Humility."

—Charles Caleb Colton

Tonight we wish for all people
to have access to dental care.

"Nationally, 30 percent of low-income children
received no dental care ... nearly 60 percent
failed to receive recommended
minimum levels of care."

—Kenney, Ko, and Ormond,
*New Federalism: National Survey
of America's Families*

We wish to stretch ourselves.

"The first step in breaking out of bondage
is to protest—to say 'no!' The saying of 'no!'
by an individual who has habitually acquiesced
in oppression releases energy in itself."

—Vicki Noble, *Motherpeace*

JULY
25

Our wish for the world tonight
is for everyone to find time to run fast.

"All of them say 'Run along! I'm busy as can be.'
Every one says, 'Run along, There's a little darling!'
If I'm a little darling, why don't they run with me?"

—A.A. Milne, *Come Out with Me*

JULY
26

We wish to learn to go with the flow.

"...when we have a clear and direct vision that
every part of our being is in change, in transformation,
then we begin to let go of our
most deeply conditioned attachments, and
we come into harmony with the flow."

—Joseph Goldstein,
The Experience of Insight

We wish tonight
to listen to each other.

"The greatest motivational act one person can do
for another is to listen."

—Roy E. Moody

Our wish tonight is for all of us to be aware of our motivations.

"Who dwells in his inner self, and is the same
in pleasure and pain; to whom gold or stones on earth
are one ... who is beyond both praise and blame,
and whose mind is steady and quiet."

—The Bhagavad Gita 14:24

Our wish for the world tonight
is for everyone to learn peacefulness.

"Peace is not an absence of war, it is a virtue,
a state of mind, a disposition for benevolence,
confidence, justice."

—Baruch Spinoza

JULY

30

Tonight we wish for an end
to domestic violence.

"All violence, all that is dreary and repels,
is not power, but the absence of power."

—Ralph Waldo Emerson

We wish tonight for an end
to oppression in China.

"Can a nation be free if it oppresses other nations?
It cannot."

—Vladimir Ilyich Lenin

1

We wish for everyone
to pray for their friends.

"The glory of friendship is not the outstretched hand,
nor the kindly smile, nor the joy of companionship;
it is the spiritual inspiration that comes to one when
he discovers that someone else believes in him and
is willing to trust him with his friendship."

—Ralph Waldo Emerson

2

Our wish for the world tonight is to sing.

"What do you do for your living? Are you forgiving, giving shelter? Follow your heart, love will find you, truth will unbind you. Sing out a song of the soul."

—Cris Williamson, *Song of the Soul*

3

Tonight we wish to remember
to be thankful for what we have.

"Thanks be to God for his inexpressible gift!"

—II Corinthians 15, *Holy Bible*
Revised Standard Version

4

*Our wish for the world tonight
is to end animal neglect.*

"What we have, then, is a flock of cats that have
no reason at all to trust us or to like us
even a little bit. All humans who come from
this house must be bad news to them, or at least
are not harbingers of good news like
food and concern."

—Roger A. Caras,
A Cat Is Watching

Our wish tonight
is to eliminate child poverty
in the United States.

"One in six children in the United States
lives in poverty."

—National Center for
Children in Poverty

Tonight we wish
to help Afghan refugees.

"Afghans now constitute the largest
refugee population in the world, with estimates
of up to 4 million living abroad and
hundreds of thousands more displaced
within their own country."

—Doctors without Borders/
Medecins sans Frontieres

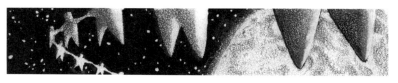

7

We wish all people
get to grow flowers.

"Flowers have a mysterious and subtle influence
upon the feelings."

—Henry Ward Beecher

8

*Our wish for the world tonight
is that people stop doing violence
in the name of God.*

"It is the conviction that wrong worship is the sum
of evil, that power, or race, or state, or creed,
improperly exalted above God,
spell the human wasteland."

—Kenneth Cragg, *The House of Islam*

We wish to be more aware
of our use of water.

"In the next 50 years, an additional 3 billion people
are expected to inhabit the Earth, creating even more
demand for water for drinking, irrigation, and
industry ... most groundwater is still pristine,
but unless we take immediate action,
clean groundwater will not be there
when we need it."

—Payal Sampat, *Deep Trouble:
The Hidden Threat of Groundwater*

We wish tonight to let go
of any desire to have power
over others.

"Resistance challenges power-over by confronting it
with speech and actions that embody a reality
incongruent with that of the authorities."

—Starhawk, *Truth or Dare*

Our wish for the world
is for all of us to nurture the power
within ourselves.

"You are here to enable the divine purpose
of the universe to unfold.
That is how important you are!"

—Eckhart Tolle, *The Power of Now*

12

Tonight we wish for everyone
to experience the earth as sacred.

"Thou art the mother-womb,
The one who creates Mankind."

—Old Babylonian Text,
*An Anthology of Sacred Texts by
and About Women*, edited by Serinity Young

We wish to save the endangered Black Rhinos.

"During the last 40 years Africa's black rhino population has fallen from an estimated 100,000 to only 2,700. Now every individual counts and we must do all we can to secure their future."

—Care for the Wild International

We wish to learn at least one other language.

"If you talk to a man in a language he understands,
that goes to his head. If you talk to him in
his language, that goes to his heart."

—Nelson Mandela

We wish that people
around the world
will stand against hatred.

"We cannot overcome anger and hatred simply
by suppressing them. *We need to actively cultivate
the antidotes to hatred: patience and tolerance.*"

—The Dalai Lama,
The Art of Happiness

16

*Our wish for the world
is that we find ways to distribute
the world's wealth more evenly.*

"The cornucopia of resources that are being extracted,
mined, and exhausted are so poorly distributed that
20 percent of the earth's people are chronically
hungry or starving, while the rest of the population,
largely in the North, control and consume
80 percent of the world's wealth."

—Paul Hawken,
The Ecology of Commerce

17

Tonight we wish that every child
has at least one good pair of shoes.

"Children who live in poverty and have grossly
inadequate shoes and clothing can't concentrate
on learning. Instead, they are cold because
they have no sweaters or jackets. They are in
physical pain because the shoes they wear
every day are far too small, or far too big."

—Shoes That Fit

AUGUST
18

We wish to learn humility.

"Fullness of knowledge always means
some understanding of the depths of our ignorance;
and then is always conducive to humility
and reverence."

—Robert Millikan

Tonight we wish for
all nations, institutions, and people
to cultivate diversity.

"If we are to achieve a richer culture, rich in
contrasting values, we must recognize the whole
gamut of human potentialities, and so weave a less
arbitrary social fabric, one in which each diverse
human gift will find a fitting place."

—Margaret Mead

20

*Our wish for the world tonight
is for all of us to have the opportunity
to follow our dreams.*

"All our dreams can come true,
if we have the courage to pursue them."

—Walt Disney

21

Tonight we wish for everyone,
including ourselves,
to learn generosity.

"He who allows his day to pass by without practicing
generosity and enjoying life's pleasures is like
a blacksmith's bellows: he breathes
but does not live."

—Indian Proverb

Our wish for the world tonight
is for those who wish to hurt others
to find compassion in their hearts.

"Make no judgements where you
have no compassion."

—Anne McCaffrey

Our wish for the world tonight
is to save the endangered
muriqui monkey.

"This time there is no place to call Ground Zero.
Every continent is Ground Zero;
Earth is Ground Zero."

—John Weiner, *The Next One Hundred Years,*
Shaping the Fate of Our Living Earth

We wish to experience
the sacredness of rivers.

"The ecological problems of modern society are
to a large extent the result of two factors:
fragmentation within the cultural system and a lack
of harmony with nature.... Sacred places are
touchstones for personal and cultural renewal."

—James A. Swan, *Sacred Places*

25

Tonight we wish for all children
to get an adequate education.

"No one has yet fully realized the wealth of sympathy,
kindness, and generosity hidden in the soul of a child.
The effort of every true education should be
to unlock that treasure."

—Emma Goldman, *Living My Life*

*Our wish tonight is
to always remember to turn out
the lights when we leave a room.*

"The 50 million people who will be added to
the U.S. population over the next forty years
will have approximately the same global impact
in terms of resource consumption as
2 billion people in India."

—Paul Hawken,
The Ecology of Commerce

27

Our wish for the world tonight
is for people around the world
to pray for their enemies,
not against them.

"You have heard it said, 'You shall love your neighbor
and hate your enemy.' But I say to you,
Love your enemies and pray for those who
persecute you, so that you may be sons of your Father;
who is in heaven...."

—Matthew 5:43–45, *The Holy Bible,*
Revised Standard Version

We wish to be flexible.

"You have to be flexible. If you have a plan
and just blindly follow it, it's worse than
no plan at all."

—L.F. McCollum

Tonight we wish for us all
to be able to see beyond
our own concerns.

"It's as though you reach out with your eyes
a little further each day. Try literally doing that
when you get up in the morning; try throwing
your eyes and your heart out into the universe."

—Sun Bear, *The Path of Power*

We wish to learn to better
differentiate our wants
from our needs.

"We always try to accumulate more and more, and
we think these 'cows' are essential for our existence.
In fact, they may be the obstacles that prevent us
from being happy. Release your cows and
become a free person."

—Thich Nhat Hahn,
The Heart of the Buddha's Teaching

31

We wish tonight to find ways
to purify ourselves.

"The mother earth has special places
to cleanse your body, mind, and spirit."

—Wallace Black Elk

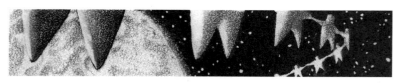

1

We wish to more fully
accept ourselves.

"Make it a habit to ask yourself:
What's going on inside me at this moment?
The question will point you in the right direction.
But don't analyze, just watch.
Focus your attention within.
Feel the energy of the emotion.
If there is no emotion present, take your attention
more deeply into the inner energy field of your body.
It is the doorway into Being."

—Eckhart Tolle, *The Power of Now*

2

*Our wish for the world tonight
is for all who are ill
to get the medicine they need.*

"One-third of the world's population lacks access
to essential drugs to treat life threatening diseases,
including AIDS. In the most impoverished parts
of the world that number is more than 50%."

—International Gay and Lesbian
Human Rights Commission

3

Tonight we wish for everyone
to have paper to write on.

"I would love to spend all my time writing to you;
I'd love to share with you all that goes through
my mind, all that weighs on my heart,
all that gives air to my soul...."

—Luigi Pirandello

4

We wish we will always
stand up for others.

"It is from numberless diverse acts of courage and
belief that human history is shaped. Each time
a man stands up for an ideal, or acts to improve
the lot of others or strikes out against injustice,
he sends forth a tiny ripple of hope."

—Robert F. Kennedy

5

Tonight we wish to learn to
stand up for ourselves.

"Life is not easy for any of us. But what of that?
We must have perseverance and above all confidence
in ourselves. We must believe that we are gifted
for something and this thing must be attained."

—Marie Curie

Our wish for the world tonight
is for an end to poverty
in Great Britain.

"The U.K. figures reveal how widespread poverty
has become in Britain—more than half the population
can expect to be touched by it at any one time."

—Organization for Economic
Cooperation and Development

7

Tonight we wish for all of us
to be able to grow fresh herbs.

"A herb garden is the perfect place of peace to relax
after a stressful day. This enchanted place has
an uncanny combination of beauty
and usefulness...."

—companyofwolves.org

8

*Our wish for the world
is for everyone to remember
that life is about change.*

"Of course there is no formula for success except,
perhaps, an unconditional acceptance
of life and what it brings."

—Arthur Rubinstein

We wish to always be aware that
the people we encounter everyday
are as human as we are.

"Constant kindness can accomplish much.
As the sun makes ice melt, kindness causes
misunderstanding, mistrust, and hostility
to evaporate."

—Albert Schweitzer

We wish tonight to be resolute.

"Determination gives you the resolve
to keep going in spite of the road blocks
that lay before you."

—Dennis Waitley

11

Tonight we wish for the world
that we may all recognize
that every little thing is really part
of one great thing.

"How have I been able to live so long outside Nature
without identifying myself with it? Everything lives,
moves, everything corresponds; the magnetic rays,
emanating either from myself or others,
cross the limitless chain of created things...."

—Gerard De Nerval, *Selected Writings*
edited by Geoffrey Wagner

12

Our wish for the world tonight
is for all of us to be able
to spend time alone.

"...I find there is a quality to being alone
that is incredibly precious. Life rushes back into
the void, richer, more vivid, fuller than before.
It is as if in parting one did actually lose an arm.
And then, like the star-fish, one grows it anew;
one is whole again, complete and round—
more whole, even, than before, when
the other people had pieces of one."

—Anne Morrow Lindbergh,
Gift from the Sea

We wish for all people
to have access to adequate
mental health care.

"Six out of every seven mentally ill persons
in the United States receive
inadequate treatment for their illness...."

—*Journal of General Medicine*

14

*Our wish for the world tonight
is that people not drink
too much alcohol.*

"As you develop dependence on alcohol,
you also develop 'blindness'—a defense system
that allows you to ignore the problem."

—Robert M. Morse, M.D.

15

We wish to learn from our choices.

"The strongest principle of growth
lies in the human choice."

—George Eliot, *Daniel Deronda*

16

We wish tonight to realize
that there is more than one way
to do a thing.

"We put our truths together in pieces,
but you use nails, and I use glue.
You mend with staples. I mend with screws.
You stitch what I would bandage.
Your truth may not look like mine,
but that is not what matters.
What matters is this:
you can look at a scar and see hurt or
you can look at a scar and see healing."

—Sheri Reynolds

17

*Our wish for the world tonight
is for all people to see
the global picture
as clearly as possible.*

"The value of having an inner map of the world as it is
(not as it's broadcast) is this: it allows you to know
that your task is larger than yourself.
If you choose, just by virtue of being a decent person,
you are entrusted with passing on something of value
through a dark and crazy time—"

—Michael Ventura

18

We wish to be free from shame.

"We first crush people to the earth, and then claim
the right of trampling on them forever
because they are prostrate."

—Lydia Maria Child

19

Tonight we wish to clarify
our sense of purpose.

"The first principle of ethical power is Purpose.
By purpose, I don't mean your objective or
intention—something toward which you are
always striving. Purpose is something bigger.
It is the picture you have of yourself—
the kind of person you want to be."

—Kenneth Blanchard

20

*Our wish tonight
is to explore and heal our pain.*

"We are not born all at once, but by bits.
The body first, and the spirit later,
and the birth and growth of the spirit,
in those who are attentive to their own inner life,
are slow and exceedingly painful.
Our mothers are racked with the pains of
our physical birth; we ourselves
suffer the longer pains of our spiritual growth."

—Mary Antin

21

We wish tonight for all of us
to acknowledge that we are
a part of our ecosystem.

"The first law of ecology is that everything
is related to everything else."

—Barry Commoner

We wish that all people
may finish High School
or the equivalent.

"All who have meditated on the art of
governing mankind have been convinced that
the fate of empires depends on
the education of youth."

—Aristotle

23

*Our wish for the world tonight
is that everyone will celebrate
the ways we connect with others.*

"The more we take the welfare of others to heart and
work for their benefit, the more benefit we derive
for ourselves. This is a fact we can see.
And the more selfish we remain and self-centered,
the more selfish our way of life is,
the lonelier we feel and more miserable.
This is also a fact we can see."

—The Dalai Lama

Tonight we wish to use less oil.

"Now try to imagine 450 million automobiles on
the road today, the railroads and trucks, the tractors
and heavy equipment, the chainsaws and motorcycles,
the diesel fuel for ships, the jet fuel for airplanes, and
to them add the oil- and coal-fired turbines
generating 1 million megawatts of electricity,
the thousands of steel works fed with coke,
the natural gasoline flared at petroleum well-heads
and burned on our stovetops."

—Paul Hawken,
The Ecology of Commerce

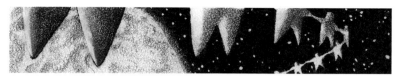

25

We wish for the world
that people will find the courage
to take reasonable chances.

"Living at risk is jumping off the cliff and
building your wings on the way down."

—Ray Bradbury

26

We wish tonight
to learn the art of contemplation.

"Leisure is a form of silence, not noiselessness.
It is the silence of contemplation such as occurs
when we let our minds rest on a rosebud,
a child at play, a Divine mystery,
or a waterfall."

—Bishop Fulton J. Sheen

Our wish for the world tonight
is for all of us to learn
to be good sports.

"One man practicing good sportsmanship is far better
than a hundred teaching it."

—Knute Rockne

28

Tonight we wish for the world that suffering will be alleviated in Russia.

"More than two-thirds of births in Russia are marred by complications.... The number of normal births declined from 45.3 percent in 1992 to just 30 percent last year, said Olga Frolova, head of the statistics department of Russia's Academy of Medical Science. She attributed the decline to the spread of heavy drinking and drug use, complications caused by sexually transmitted disease, and the nation's overall worsening health."

—Associated Press, October 5, 2000

29

We wish to always
admit responsibility for our actions.

"Act, if you like, but you do it at your peril.
Men's actions are too strong for them.
Show me a man who has acted and who has not
been the victim and slave of his action."

—Ralph Waldo Emerson

30

Tonight we wish that parents
will apologize to their children
whenever they are wrong.

"Learning is the result of listening, which in turn
leads to even better listening and attentiveness
to the other person. In other words,
to learn from the child, we must have empathy
and empathy grows as we learn."

—Alice Miller, *For Your Own Good*

1

We wish to free ourselves
from our old irrational fears.

"Fear always distorts our perception and confuses us
as to what is going on. Love is the total absence
of fear. Love asks no questions. Its natural state is
one of extension and expansion, not comparison
and measurement."

—Gerald Jampolsky, M.D.,
Love Is Letting Go of Fear

2

Tonight we wish for adults
to jump more often.

"You will jump out of the pitch of this house,
It will be a holiday, a parade, a fiesta!
Then you'll fly."

—Anne Sexton,
A Little Uncomplicated Hymn

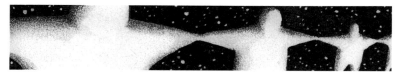

*Our wish tonight
is to fight anger with compassion.*

"When we are angry, our tendency is to punish
the other person. But when we do, there is
only an escalation of the suffering.
The Buddah proposed that instead
you send her a gift."

—Thich Nhat Hanh,
The Heart of the Buddha's Teaching

4

*Our wish for the world tonight
is that we may all learn
to honor death.*

"How disbelieve ye in Allah when ye were dead
and He gave life to you! Then he will give you death,
then life again, and then unto Him ye will return."

—Al Baqarah 2:28.21, *The Koran*

We wish tonight for all people
to have access to adequate
medical care.

"A community is democratic only when
the humblest and weakest person can enjoy
the highest civil, economic, and social rights
that the biggest and most powerful possess."

—A. Philip Randolph

6

We wish to learn patience.

"Learn the art of patience. Apply discipline to
your thoughts when they become anxious over
the outcome of a goal. Impatience breeds anxiety,
fear, discouragement and failure. Patience creates
confidence, decisiveness and a rational outlook,
which eventually leads to success."

—Brian Adams

Tonight we wish
to be open to grace.

"We do not come to grace; grace comes to us.
Try as we might to obtain grace, it may yet elude us.
We may seek it not yet it will find us."

—M. Scott Peck, M.D.,
The Road Less Traveled

OCTOBER
8

Our wish for the world tonight
is for all people to accept
one another.

"If you see good in people, you radiate a harmonious,
loving energy which uplifts those around you.
If you can maintain this habit
this energy will turn into
a steady flow of love."

—Annamalai Swami

9

We wish tonight to recognize
the simple choices we make daily.

"One's philosophy is not expressed in words;
it is expressed in the choices one makes....
In the long run, we shape our lives and
will shape ourselves. The process
never ends until we die."

—Eleanor Roosevelt

10

*Our wish for the world tonight
is that more people around the world
will stand for justice.*

"The dead cannot cry out for justice;
it is the duty of the living to do so for them."

—Lois McMaster Bujold,
Diplomatic Immunity

Tonight we wish that everyone
around the world
will have access to pencils and pens.

"The pen is the tongue of the mind."

—Miguel de Cervantes

12

We wish tonight for all of us
to learn to appreciate solitude.

"It is easy in the world to live after
the world's opinion; it is easy in solitude
to live after our own; but the great man
is he who in the midst of the crowd
keeps with perfect sweetness
the independence of solitude."

—Ralph Waldo Emerson, *Self Reliance*

Tonight we wish that people
will no longer live for vengeance.

"Something of vengeance I had tasted for
the first time; as aromatic wine it seemed,
on swallowing, warm and racy; its after-flavour,
metallic and corroding, gave me a sensation
as if I had been poisoned."

—Charlotte Bronte

We wish for the world
for all people to free themselves
from feeling victimized.

"What I see without is a reflection of what I have
first seen within my own mind....
I always project onto the world the thoughts,
feelings and attitudes which pre-occupy me.
I can see the world differently
by changing my mind about
what I want to see."

—Gerald G. Jampolsky, M.D.,
Love Is Letting Go of Fear

*Our wish for the world tonight
is for everyone of us to appreciate
the natural world.*

"Climb the mountains and get their good tidings.
Nature's peace will flow into you
as sunshine flows into trees.
The winds will blow their freshness into you,
and the storms their energy,
while cares will drop like autumn leaves."

—John Muir, *Our National Parks*

Tonight we wish for everyone,
all over the world,
to experience a beach as sacred.

"The sea does not reward those who are too anxious,
too greedy, or too impatient: One should lie empty,
open, choiceless as a beach—
waiting for the gift from the sea."

—Anne Morrow Lindbergh,
Gift from the Sea

OCTOBER

17

*Our wish for the world
is for harmony between nations.*

"Observe good faith and justice toward all nations.
Cultivate peace and harmony with all....
The nation which indulges toward another
an habitual hatred or an habitual fondness
is in some degree a slave. It is a slave to
its animosity or to its affection, either of which
is sufficient to lead it astray
from its duty and its interest."

—George Washington, Farewell Address,
17 September, 1796

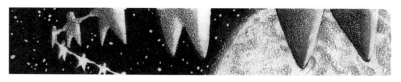

We wish tonight to abandon greed.

"There is no calamity greater than lavish desires.
There is no greater guilt than discontentment.
And there is no greater disaster than greed."

—Lau-tzu, *The Way of Lau-tzu*

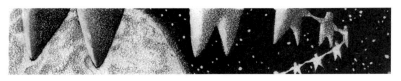

19

Our wish for the world tonight is to learn to honor our life changes.

"There are as many worlds as there are kinds of days,
and as an opal changes its colors and its fire
to match the nature of the day,
so do I."

—John Steinbeck

Tonight our wish for the world
is for an end to suffering
in Central America.

"May we remember, as we log on, that half
the world's people have never used a telephone,
and recall, as we chatter, that most of those around us
have no chance to speak or move as they choose.
May we recall that more than half a million beings
live without food, and that as many children
live amidst poverty and war."

—Pico Iyer

We wish tonight to work in some way
to save all endangered species.

"Over 5,000 animal species worldwide are currently
classified as endangered, due to habitat destruction,
commercial exploitation, damage caused by
intrusion of non-native animals and pollution.
Survival of ecosystems depends on biodiversity,
or variety of plants, animals and habitat.
This means that the removal of one species
through extinction can jeopardize
the entire ecosystem."

—ecoworld.com

We wish to always be able to see
the big picture.

"Bell's theorem demands that we rethink
the conventional scientific ideas of the nature
of the material world ... the metaphor of the dance
illustrates that everything is connected,
communicating instantaneously all the time.
This system of communicating parts included you
and me—we are all an integral part
of the whole dance of life."

—Paula Payne Hardin,
*What Are You Doing
with the Rest of Your Life?*

*Our wish for the world tonight
is to free ourselves of self-loathing.*

"The problem with most people is that
they live their lives and never discover that the Judge
and the Victim rule their mind,
therefore they don't have a chance to be free.
The first step toward personal freedom is awareness.
We need to be aware that we are not free
in order to be free."

—Don Miguel Ruiz,
The Four Agreements

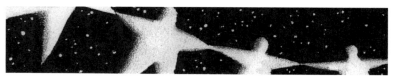

OCTOBER

24

We wish for all people
to take good care of their teeth.

"The important thing to remember is that an effective
brushing cleans every exposed tooth surface
in a gently, massaging motion ... most people think
they brush for at least a minute or two, but in reality
they brush for 30 seconds or less.
Time yourself and see how you do.
An effective brushing takes 2–3 minutes."

—healthyteeth.org

Tonight we wish that everyone
will get the chance to run far.

"Something in me wanted to find out
how far I could run without stopping."

—Jacki Hanson

*Our wish for the world
is that we not forget how to giggle.*

"All you need in the world is love and laughter.
That's all anybody needs. To have love in one hand
and laughter in the other."

—August Wilson,
Famous Black Quotations

OCTOBER

27

Tonight we wish for
an end to poverty in India.

"The poverty of our century is unlike that
of any other. It is not, as poverty was before, the result
of natural scarcity, but of a set of priorities
imposed upon the rest of the world by the rich."

—John Berger, *In Keeping a Rendevous*

Our wish for the world is to do more
to stop polluting the world's rivers.

"Fresh water is a precious resource and the increasing
pollution of our rivers and lakes is a cause for alarm."

—Young People's Trust for the Environment

We wish to volunteer our time
to help others.

"As each has received a gift, employ it for
one another, as good stewards of God's varied grace:
whoever speaks, as one who utters oracles of God;
whoever renders service, as one who renders it
by the strength which God supplies..."

—1 Peter 4: 10–11, *The Holy Bible,*
Revised Standard Version

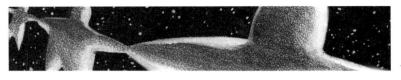

Tonight we wish for all people
to work to end suffering in the world.

"As long as space endures
As long as sentient beings remain
May I too live
To dispel the miseries of the world."

—The Dalai Lama,
The Art of Happiness

*Our wish for the world tonight
is for the survival of the Giant Panda.*

"In spite of efforts on several fronts, conservation
efforts to save the giant panda continue to be
hindered by the loss of and change within the panda's
habitat in the mountains of China....
The report calls for urgent action to support
creation of habitat corridors to link isolated
panda populations and urges the Chinese government
to establish a permanent fund to combat
chronic financial shortages in panda reserves."

—Report from
the World Wildlife Fund

1

Tonight we wish to celebrate love.

"The ripening journey brings us to love of giving, and
the blossoming of higher values, such as compassion,
forgiveness, and altruism. Finally there is
the direct experience of spirit itself,
which is pure love. The journey climaxes
in the same knowledge that a baby began with,
although it couldn't voice that knowledge:
I am love."

—Deepak Chopra,
The Path to Love

2

We wish to learn to
better pick our battles.

"We've all got to remember to pick our battles
carefully, to be prepared to lose small ones,
and to hold out for big ones."

—Marge Kennedy and
Janet Spencer King,
The Single Parent Family

3

Our wish for the world tonight
is for all people everywhere
to celebrate peace.

"Christ has called us to new visions
Here to celebrate and praise,
Here confess our old divisions,
Here our peace petitions raise.
Come repentant, come forgiving,
Come in joy and hope and prayer.
Christ, once crucified, now living,
Bids us faith and love to share."

—Jane Parker Herber, *A Singing Faith*

4

Tonight we wish for
more active conservation of
the world's wild lions.

"While the cat-conservation world was worried
about the fate of Asia's endangered tigers,
lions—considered vulnerable but not endangered—
were quietly slipping toward oblivion."

—Terry McCarthy, *Nowhere to Roam*

5

We wish tonight for all parents
to set appropriate limits
for their children.

"It is our continuing love for our children that
makes us want them to become all they can be,
and their continuing love for us that
helps them accept healthy discipline—
from us and eventually from themselves."

—Fred Rogers,
Mister Rogers Talks with Parents

6

*Our wish tonight is for everyone
to have a chance to go to college.*

"The ability to think straight, some knowledge
of the past, some vision of the future,
some skill to do useful service, some urge
to fit that service into the well-being of
the community—these are
the most vital things
education must try to produce."

—Virginia Gildersleeve

7

We wish to always appreciate
the beauty of every stream
and creek.

"The creeks ... are an active mystery,
fresh every minute. Theirs is the mystery
of continuous creation and all that
providence implies: the uncertainty of vision,
the horror of the fixed, the dissolution of the present,
the intricacy of beauty, the pressure of fecundity,
the elusiveness of the free, and
the flawed nature of perfection."

—Annie Dillard,
Pilgrim at Tinker Creek

8

Tonight we wish to always
reach a little higher.

"In the mountains of truth, you never climb in vain.
Either you already reach a higher point today,
or you exercise your strength in order to be able
to climb higher tomorrow."

—Friedrich Wilhelm Nietzsche

9

Our wish for the world tonight
is for people to never forget
how to hop.

"Christopher Robin goes
Hoppity, hoppity.
Hoppity, hopitty, hop.
Whenever I tell him
Politely to stop it he
Says he can't possibly stop."

—A.A. Milne, *Hoppity*

10

Our wish for the world tonight is for the preservation of the Blue Whale.

"The blue whale is the world's largest living animal.
In the northern hemisphere, these leviathans reach
70 to 80 feet in length and weigh up to
200,000 pounds.... Between 1910 and 1966,
approximately 8,200 were killed in the North Pacific,
severely reducing the population.
The North Pacific population is now estimated at
1,200 to 1,700 animals; the worldwide population
is estimated at 8,000 to 12,000."

—Alaska Department of Fish and Game
Division of Wildlife Conservation

11

Tonight we wish for
houses for the homeless.

"Once again, we've wasted time and money by dealing
with the homeless backward. Too much energy
has gone into deciding where we do not
want them to be, and making sure
that they would not be there."

—Anna Quindlen, *Thinking Out Loud*

12

We wish tonight for all of us
to believe that we are worthwhile.

"...By telling them that we know they have a problem
and we know they can solve it, we can pass on
a realistic attitude as well as empower our children
with self confidence and a sense of their own worth."

—Barbara Coloroso, *Kids Are Worth It*

13

*Our wish for the world tonight
is for all people to be able
to make new friends.*

"Friendship demands a religious treatment.
We talk of choosing our friends,
but friends are self-elected.
Reverence is a great part of it."

—Ralph Waldo Emerson, *Friendship*

14

We wish for every one
to feel safe in his home.

"When society comes to value one child truly....
There will be safety. There will be the chance
to be well, to be sure; room to grow and breathe in;
the sacred privacy of the home circle—all those things
that are the birthright of every child.
And there will be, in some way, beauty
to which the soul of the child naturally turns,
as does a plant to light."

—Albion Fellows Bacon,
Beauty for Ashes

15

Our wish for the world tonight
is to someday make peaceful contact
with beings on another planet.

"Perhaps when distant people on other planets
pick up some wave-length of ours
all they hear is a continuous scream."

—Iris Murdoch, *Message to the Planet*

16

Tonight we wish that all children
waiting to be adopted
will find loving families.

"What is a neglected child? He is a child
not planned for, not wanted. Neglect begins,
therefore, before he is born."

—Pearl S. Buck,
Children for Adoption

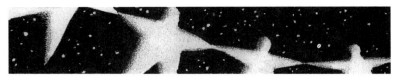

17

We wish tonight for
an end to all violent crime.

"Violence shapes and obsesses our society,
and if we do not stop being violent
we have no future."

—Edward Bond, *Lear*

18

We wish all people
will have the opportunity
to learn to play a sport.

"It's about learning your craft.
That's a wonderful thing—especially with today's
consumerism and instant gratification.
You can't buy that. It's about making decisions,
corrections, choices. I don't think it's
so much about becoming a tennis player.
It's about becoming a person."

—Billie Jean King

We wish to remember
to behave respectfully
towards all people.

"'Walk a mile in my shoes' is good advice.
Our children will learn to respect others if they are
used to imagining themselves in another's place."

—Neil Kurshan,
Raising Your Child to Be a Mensch

Tonight we wish for all of us
to be happy just to be ourselves.

"Know how to live within yourself: there is
in your soul a whole world of mysterious
and enchanted thoughts; they will be drowned
by the noise without; daylight will drive them away:
listen to their singing and be silent."

—Fyodor Tyutchev, *Silentium*

21

We wish to trust our intuition.

"The only really valuable thing is intuition."

—Albert Einstein

22

Tonight we wish for all of us
to learn to respect ourselves.

"But it's important, while we are supporting lessons
in respecting others, to remember that many of
our youngest kids need to learn to respect themselves.
You learn your worth from the way you are treated."

—Anna Quindlen

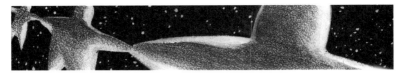

23

*Our wish for the world tonight
is for ways to be found
to restore the health of our families.*

"The family is both the fundamental unit of society
as well as the root of culture. It represents
a child's initial source of unconditional love
and acceptance and provides a lifelong
connectedness with others."

—Marianne E. Neifert, M.D.,
Dr. Mom's Parenting Guide

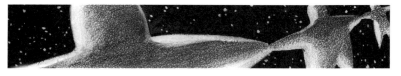

24

We wish to remember that
there will always be difficulties
to overcome in our lives.

"If I had a formula for bypassing trouble,
I would not pass it around.
Trouble creates a capacity to handle it.
I don't embrace trouble; that's as bad as
treating it as an enemy. But I do say
meet it as a friend, for you'll see a lot of it
and had better be on speaking terms with it."

—Oliver Wendell Holmes

We wish tonight for each of us
to experience awe.

"Let your soul go free for a moment into that scene
outside your window ... and there encounter
gape-jawed and silent, the God of birds and
birth defects, trees and cancer, quarks and galaxies,
earthquakes and supernovas, awesome, edifying,
dreadful and good, more beautiful and
more terrible than is strictly necessary.
Let it strike you dumb with worship and fear,
beyond words, beyond logic."

—Chet Raymo

26

*Our wish for the world is
for everyone to be able to cultivate
and protect the right to speak freely.*

"Without free speech no search for truth is possible ...
no discovery of truth is useful.... Better a thousandfold
abuse of free speech than denial of free speech.
The abuse dies in a day but the denial
slays the life of the people,
and entombs the hope of the race."

—Charles Bradlaugh

27

We wish to retain
our natural curiosity.

"I think, at a child's birth, if a mother could ask
a fairygodmother to endow it with the most useful gift,
that gift would be curiosity."

—Eleanor Roosevelt

28

Tonight we wish to allow ourselves
to daydream sometimes.

"The only big ideas I've ever had
have come from daydreaming, but modern life
keeps people from daydreaming.
Every moment of the day your mind is being occupied,
controlled, by some one else at school, at work,
watching television. Getting away from that
is important. You need to just kick back in a chair
and let your mind daydream."

—Paul MacCready

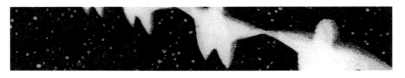

We wish for all of us
to enjoy our grandparents.

"Nobody can do for little children
what grandparents do.
Grandparents sort of sprinkle stardust
over the lives of little children."

—Alex Haley

30

Our wish for the world
is for each of us to seek repentance
when we need it.

"Of all acts of man repentance is the most divine.
The greatest of all faults is to be
conscious of none."

—Thomas Carlyle

1

Tonight we wish for everyone
to have a healthy body.

"The greatest of follies is to sacrifice health
for any other kind of happiness."

—Arthur Schopenhauer

2

We wish that all people
will take care of one another.

"What is compassion? It is not simply a sense
of sympathy or caring for the person suffering,
not simply a warmth of heart toward the person
before you, or a sharp clarity of recognition
of their needs and pain, it is also a sustained and
practical determination to do whatever is possible
and necessary to help alleviate their suffering."

—Sogyal Rinpoche,
Glimpse After Glimpse

3

Our wish for the world tonight
is for all of us to do something nice
for somebody else.

"Christopher Robin had a question to ask first,
and he was wondering how to ask it.
'Well,' he said at last, 'it's a very nice house,
and if your house is blown down,
you *must* go somewhere else, mustn't you, Piglet?
What would *you* do, if *your* house was blown down?'
Before Piglet could think, Pooh answered for him.
'He'd come live with me,' said Pooh,
'wouldn't you, Piglet?'"

—A.A. Milne, *The House at Pooh Corner*

4

Tonight we wish
that we all have everything we need.

"As long as we pretend that only poor or
abnormal families need outside assistance,
we will shortchange poor families, overcompensate
rich ones, and fail to come up with effective policies
for helping families in the middle."

—Stephanie Coontz

We wish to learn to expect nothing
but the unexpected.

"None of us knows what the next change is going
to be, what unexpected opportunity is just around
the corner, waiting a few months or a few years
to change all the tenor of our lives."

—Kathleen Norris, *Hands Full of Living*

6

*Our wish tonight is for everyone
to feel successful.*

"To laugh often and much; to win the respect
of intelligent people and the affection of children;
to earn the appreciation of honest critics and
endure the betrayal of false friends;
to appreciate beauty, to find the best in others;
to leave the world a little better; whether by
a healthy child, a garden patch or a redeemed
social condition; to know even one life has breathed
easier because you have lived.
This is the meaning of success."

—Ralph Waldo Emerson

7

We wish to always
help our children.

"You are the bows from which your children
as living arrows are sent forth."

—Kahlil Gibran, *The Prophet*

8

*Our wish is for everyone
to be able to shout for joy.*

"The joy that isn't shared dies young."

—Anne Sexton

9

We wish to always revere
all forms of life.

"By having a reverence for life, we enter into
a spiritual relation with the world....
By practicing reverence for life we become
good, deep, and alive."

—Albert Schweitzer

10

Our wish for the world tonight
is that we will all learn to be present
with those who are dying.

"Your stability is part of the dying person, so if you
are stable then automatically the person in the bardo
state will be attracted to that. In other words,
present a very sane and solid situation to the person
who is going to die. Just relate with him,
just open to each other simultaneously,
and develop the meeting of the two minds."

—Chogyam Trungpa Rinpoche,
The Tibetan Book of the Dead

11

Tonight we wish for
an end to unemployment in Europe.

"The precipitous rise of unemployment in Europe
has caused huge social problems in recent years.
The rupture of social cohesion, the marginalization
of a large part of the labor force and the fall of
living standards for a significant number of
European citizens has shaken the faith of
Europeans in the European ideal..."

—Theodore Pelagidis,
*European Unemployment Myths
and Realities*

12

We wish tonight to continue
to learn more about our world.

"There are grounds for cautious optimism that we may
now be near the end of the search for
the ultimate laws of nature."

—Stephen W. Hawking,
A Brief History of Time,
From the Big Bang to Black Holes

13

We wish to always tell the truth.

"Hitler had said that if you tell a big enough lie,
people will believe it, but he rather overlooked
the fact that once the lie is exposed,
everything else you've said
is also disbelieved."

—Paul Brickhill, *The Great Escape*

14

Our wish for the world tonight
is that we will all do
what we know is right.

"Real integrity is doing the right thing, knowing that
nobody's going to know whether you did it or not."

—Oprah Winfrey

We wish tonight
to be careful with our words.

"Words are, of course, the most powerful drug
used by mankind."

—Rudyard Kipling

16

Tonight we wish for
a cure for cystic fibrosis.

"According to the Cystic Fibrosis Foundation's
National Patient Registry, the median age of survival
for a person with CF is 33.4 years.
As more advances have been made
in the treatment of CF,
the number of adults with CF has steadily grown."

—Cystic Fibrosis Foundation

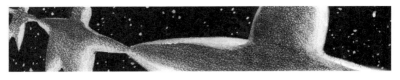

17

Tonight we wish for
each of us to keep an open mind.

"The mind is not a vessel to be filled
but a fire to be kindled."

—Plutarch

Our wish tonight is that the world could be all one country.

"It is not for him to pride himself who loveth
his own country, but rather for him who loveth
the whole world. The earth is but one country
and mankind its citizens."

—Baha'a'llah

19

Our wish for the world tonight
is for everyone to have
the courage and the right
to criticize our governments.

"I love America more than any country in this world,
and, exactly for this reason, I insist on the right
to criticize her perpetually."

—James Baldwin,
Notes of a Native Son

20

We wish to always
remain optimistic.

"No pessimist ever discovered the secret of the stars,
or sailed to an uncharted land, or opened
a new doorway for the human spirit."

—Helen Keller

21

Tonight we wish for all of us
to choose our friends carefully.

"Keep away from people who try to belittle
your ambitions. Small people always do that,
but the really great make you feel that
you, too, can become great."

—Mark Twain

Tonight we wish to find the courage
to act when we know we must.

"The true revolutionary is guided by
a great feeling of love."

—Che Guevara

*Our wish for the world tonight
is for all people to remember
that we are merely mammals.*

"But mortals suppose that the gods are born
(as they themselves are), and that they wear
men's clothing and have human voice and body.
But if cattle or lions had hands, so as to paint
their hands and produce works of art as men do,
they would paint their gods and give them
bodies in form like their own—
horses like horses, cattle like cattle."

—Xenophanes

24

Our wish tonight is for an alleviation of suffering in Asia.

"Although there has been remarkable and unprecedented progress in reducing poverty in Asia over the last 25 years, the continent still accounts for three quarters of the world's poor."

—Canadian International
Development Agency

Tonight we wish for peace on earth.

"Peace is not a relationship of nations.
It is a condition of mind brought about by
a serenity of soul. Lasting peace can come
only to a peaceful people."

—Jawaharlal Nehru

26

*Our wish for the world tonight
is to skip sometimes.*

"I wanna walk and not run.
I wanna skip and not fall.
I wanna look at the horizon
and not see a building standing tall...."

—Marie Siedel and Marcus Hummon,
Cowboy Take Me Away

27

*Our wish for the world tonight
is for everyone to be
willing to be different.*

"Without deviation progress is not possible."

—Frank Zappa

28

Tonight we wish
to pay closer attention
to all children.

"Children have more need of models than of critics."

—Carolyn Coats

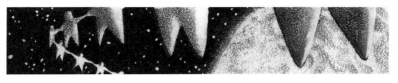

29

We wish that we may trust our path.

"We must walk consciously only part way
toward our goal, and then leap in the dark
to our success."

—Henry David Thoreau

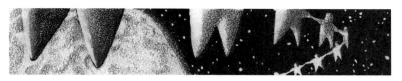

30

Tonight we wish to listen carefully
to each other's stories.

"Hearing each other's stories is a powerful way
of valuing each other.... In families and
intimate relationships, mealtimes or bedtimes
can become organic check-in times,
when each person tells the story of his or her day
without being judged or interrupted."

—Starhawk, *Truth or Dare*

31

Our wish for the world tonight is to always remember that each ending brings a new beginning.

"Life and death, then, are considered not as two separate stages, completing mankind's temporal and post-earthly existence, but as complementary places in an ever-recurring cycle; a continuity that remains unbroken...."

—Frank Waters, *Book of the Hopi*

Selected Reference List

Adams, Douglas. (1980). *The Hitchhiker's Guide to the Galaxy*. New York: Harmony Books.

Armstrong, Karen. (2001). *Buddha*. New York: Penguin Putnam.

Atwood, Margaret. (1974). *You Are Happy*. San Francisco: Harper.

Beattie, Melodie. (1990). *The Language of Letting Go: Daily Meditations for Co-Dependents*. New York: HarperCollins.

Berger, John (1992). *Keeping a Rendezvous*. New York: Vintage.

Caras, Roger. (1989). *A Cat Is Watching: A Look at the Way Cats See Us*. New York: Simon & Schuster.

Chopra, Deepak. (1996). *The Path to Love: Renewing the Power of Spirit in Your Life*. New York: Harmony Books.

Cragg, Kenneth. (1975). *The House of Islam*. Encino and Belmont: Dickenson Publishing.

Dalai Lama & Howard C. Cutler, M.D. (1998) *The Art of Happiness: A Handbook for Living.* New York: Riverhead Books.

Darcy, Rahima Baldwin. (1988). *You Are Your Child's First Teacher.* Berkeley: Celestial Arts.

Erodoes, Richard & Alfonso Ortiz (Eds.). (1984). *American Indian Myths and Legends.* New York: Pantheon.

Fischer, Louis (Ed.). (1962). *The Essential Ghandi: His Life, His Work and Ideas.* New York: Knopf and Random House.

Frost, Robert. (1936). *Selected Poems of Robert Frost.* New York: Holt, Rinehart & Winston.

Gawain, Shakti. (1993). *Living in the Light: A Personal Guide to Planetary Transformation.* New York: Bantam Books.

Gibran, Kahlil. (1923). *The Prophet.* New York: Alfred A. Knopf.

Goldstein, Joseph. (1987). *The Experience of Insight: A Simple and Direct Guide to Buddhist Meditation.* Boston: Shambhala.

Griffin, Susan. (1980). *Woman and Nature: The Roaring Inside Her.* New York: HarperCollins.

Guru Rinpoche according to the Karma Lingpa. Translated by Francesca Fremantle & Chogyam Trungpa. (1987). *The Tibetan Book of the Dead: The Great Liberation Through Hearing in the Bardo.* Boston and London: Shambala.

Hahn, Thich Nhat. (1991). *Peace Is Every Step: The Path of Mindfulness in Everyday Life.* New York: Bantam Books.

Hahn, Thich Nhat. (1996). *The Miracle of Mindfulness.* Boston: Beacon Press.

Hahn, Thich Nhat. (1998). *The Heart of the Buddha's Teaching.* Berkeley: Parallax Press.

Hahn, Thich Nhat. (2000). *The Wisdom of Thich Nhat Hahn.* New York: One Spirit.

Hammerschlag, Carl A. (1994). *The Theft of the Spirit: A Journey to Spiritual Healing.* New York: Simon & Schuster.

Hawken, Paul. (1993). *The Ecology of Commerce: A Declaration of Sustainability.* New York: HarperCollins.

The Holy Bible. Revised Standard Version.

Jampolsky, Gerald G., M.D. (1981). *Love Is Letting Go of Fear.* New York: Bantam Books.

Kabat-Zinn, Jon. (1994). *Wherever You Go There You Are: Mindfulness Meditation in Everyday Life.* New York: Hyperion.

Kema, Ayya. (May 2001). The Four Highest Emotions. *Shambala Sun,* Vol. 9, #5.

Krishnamurti, J. (1975). *Freedom from the Known.* San Francisco: Harper & Row.

Lamott, Anne. (1999). *Traveling Mercies: Some Thoughts on Faith.* New York: Pantheon Books.

Mascaro, Juan (Transl.). (1962). *The Bhagavad Gita.* New York: Penguin Books, Ltd.

McCarthy, Terry & Dorfman, Andrea (August 23, 2004). Nowhere to Roam. *Time Magazine.*

Milne, A.A. (1924). *When We Were Very Young.* New York: Dutton Children's Books.

Milne, A.A. (1926). *Winnie the Pooh.* New York: Dutton Children's Books.

Milne, A.A. (1927). *Now We Are Six.* New York: Dutton Children's Books.

Milne, A.A. (1928). *The House at Pooh Corner.* New York: Dutton Children's Books.

Mitchell, Stephen (Transl.). (1987). *The Book of Job.* San Francisco: North Point Press.

Noble, Vicki. (1983). *Motherpeace: The Way of the Goddess Through Myth, Art and Tarot.* New York: HarperCollins Publishers.

Peck, M. Scott, M.D. (1978). *The Road Less Traveled: A New Psychology of Love, Traditional Values and Spiritual Growth.* New York: Simon & Schuster, Inc.

Rapoport, Nessa. (1994). *A Woman's Book of Grieving.* New York: William Morrow & Co., Inc.

Roberts, Elizabeth & Elias Amidon (Eds.). (1991). *Earth Prayers from Around the World.* San Francisco: HaperCollins.

Ruiz, Don Miguel. (1999). *The Mastery of Love: A Practical Guide to the Art of Relationship.* San Rafael: Amber Allen Publishing.

Sarton, May. (1977). *Journal of a Solitude.* New York: W.W. Norton.

Sarton, May. (1978). *The Fur Person.* New York: W.W. Norton.

Sewell, Anna. (1907). *Black Beauty, The Autobiography of a Horse.* New York: Dodge Publishing Co.

Shakespeare, William. (1914). *As You Like It* in *The Complete Works of William Shakespeare* edited by W.J. Craig. London: Oxford University Press.

Sogyal Rinpoche. (1992). *The Tibetan Book of Living and Dying.* San Francisco: HarperSanFrancisco.

Sogyal Rinpoche. (1995). *Glimpse After Glimpse: Daily Reflections on Living and Dying.* New York: HarperCollins Publishers.

Starhawk. (1979). *The Spiral Dance: A Rebirth of the Ancient Religion of the Great Goddess.* San Francisco: Harper & Row.

Starhawk. (1990). *Truth or Dare: Encounters with Power and Authority.* San Francisco: Harper & Row.

Stevens, Wallace. (1972). *The Palm at the End of the Mind.* New York: Vintage Books.

Tolle, Eckhart. (1999). *The Power of Now: A Guide to Spiritual Enlightenment.* Novato: New World Library.

Waters, Frank. (1977). *The Book of the Hopi: The First Revelation of the Hopi's Historical and Religious World View of Life.* New York: Penguin Books.

About the Authors

Keren L. Clark was born in Charlotte, North Carolina. She graduated from Scottsdale High School in Arizona and attended Pitzer College in southern California. At Pitzer, Keren began to look beyond her conservative and Christian upbringing and to develop a social, political, and spiritual consciousness informed by a growing desire to reach out and learn more about other cultures. She spent a year abroad, learning to speak French fluently and befriending a group of Laotian and Vietnamese refugees. The experience made her particularly aware of the sufferings of people fleeing war and genocide. Back at Pitzer for her senior year, she focussed on classes in sociology, anthropology, and spirituality—a curriculum designed to deepen her understanding of human culture around the world.

Shortly after her graduation from Pitzer, Keren moved to San Francisco. While living in the Bay Area, she became involved with a spiritual collective known as "Reclaiming." She studied Wicca as a means of further expanding an already diverse spiritual foundation. In 1984, she decided to pursue a career as a Marriage and Family Therapist, enrolling in the Graduate Psychology Program at Antioch University in San Francisco. While there, she encountered Tibetan Buddhism and became more and more convinced that spirituality and a sense of belonging to a larger community are two of the core needs of all human beings. She continues to draw inspiration from Buddhist, Christian, and Wiccan sources in her own spiritual practice.

After taking her degree from Antioch in 1987, Keren became a licensed Marriage and Family Therapist. She has worked in agency settings, as well as in private practice where the cornerstone of her therapeutic technique is to guide people on their own healing journeys through a combination of spiritual and psychological techniques. Currently, she lives in Prescott, Arizona, with her three children—Ethan and Dyson, co-authors of *Wish for the World,* and Sadie.

Ethan and Dyson Posey were born at 7:00 p.m. and 7:09 p.m. respectively on December 19, 1992 in Flagstaff, Arizona. They were six and one half weeks premature and spent their first four weeks of life in the Neo-natal Intensive Care Nursery of Flagstaff Medical Center. Upon discharge, they were small but otherwise quite healthy.

The family lived in a small rural community outside of Flagstaff. The boys spent their days climbing trees, playing in the mud and ranging around the forest and high desert prairie that surrounded their home. Spirituality, tolerance and religion were frequent topics of conversation. When it was time for kindergarten, Ethan and Dyson attended a Waldorf-inspired Charter School in Flagstaff where their education focused on learning through play, the arts, literature, music and the cycles of the seasons. At school and at home, reading was always valued and regularly practiced, and by the end of third grade, each was reading at nearly the twelfth-grade level.

Ethan and Dyson are now in the sixth grade at a local Waldorf School in Prescott. According to their teacher, the twins can be counted on to help shape the moral direction of the classroom. Both boys enjoy athletics and reading. Ethan shows some promise on the violin and would like to be a NASA engineer when he grows up. Dyson aspires to be an actor and delights in entertaining his peer group.